Path of the Pearl

Path of the Pearl

· Discover Your Treasures Within ·

MARY OLSEN KELLY

BEYOND
WORDS
Publishing
I N C

Beyond Words Publishing, Inc.
20827 N.W. Cornell Road, Suite 500
Hillsboro, Oregon 97124-9808
503-531-8700

Editor: Jenefer Angell
Managing editor: Julie Steigerwaldt
Proofreader: Marvin Moore
Design: Angela Lavespere
Cover photograph: Kenny Williams
Composition: William H. Brunson Typography Services

Printed in the United States of America
Distributed to the book trade by Publishers Group West

Library of Congress Cataloging-in-Publication Data
Kelly, Mary Olsen.
        Path of the pearl : discover your treasures within / Mary Olsen Kelly.

        p.   cm.
        Includes bibliographical references.
        ISBN 1-58270-085-0
        1. Conduct of life.   2. Pearls—Miscellanea.   I. Title.
    BF637.C5 K45   2002
    158.1—dc21

                                                2002005014

The corporate mission of Beyond Words Publishing, Inc.:
    Inspire to Integrity

For Don

who taught me that whenever difficulties occur,
"This could be a pearl in the making."

Contents

$\mathcal{T}$he pearl is a living legacy of nature, each one different—just like human beings. And like us, though they may seem fragile, pearls are surprisingly strong. *Path of the Pearl* celebrates the life of the pearl as a metaphor for our own lives, sharing wisdom garnered by absorbing and transforming the bumps in the road of life. Far beyond jewelry for personal adornment, the pearl is a symbol of enlightenment; it connects us with heaven above and the power of our subconscious mind. This book is an investigation into the pearl as a form of spiritual teaching and a tool for personal growth as well as a tribute to its mystical essence and enduring allure.

I was inspired to write this book after seeing the transformational effect that pearls have had on me and on the people in my life. For the past thirteen years I have had the honor of living and working with thousands upon thousands of pearls. As co-owner with my husband, Don, of the

Black Pearl Gallery fine jewelry stores in Hawaii, I have traveled to farms on remote South Seas islands to observe how pearls are born, I have attended worldwide conferences, and I have worked with the top jewelers in the field creating original jewelry designs to enhance the pearls. Don and I attend the annual auctions in Tahiti and experience the thrill of viewing and grading thousands of pearls before deciding which farm lots we will attempt to buy.

We have known the pleasure of purchasing large quantities of pearls, bringing them back home, and sitting in a room filled with their rainbow-colors glowing before us. We have made friends with people who work in all areas of the pearl world: farming pearls, tending pearls, selling pearls, and creating jewelry to showcase pearls.

It has been my desire to learn as much as possible about this amazing gem. I have read about pearls, researched them, learned to determine their value and worth. In the course of learning about pearls, I have fallen deeply under their spell. And I have been blessed to receive their teachings. Pearls have taught me about beauty, rarity, and nature's wisdom and bounty. They have also taught me about life and about people, and they have given me countless insights into myself. I have found that the criteria by which we evaluate the quality of a pearl—shape, size, color, luster, orient, and perfection—correspond to human characteristics such as courage, faith, trust, resolve, hope, and love, and they can be used as a guide for evaluating and improving the quality of our lives.

I have seen hundreds of people fall in love with pearls. I have seen the look of recognition cross a customer's face upon discovering their "perfect" pearl, a joy comparable to finding a long-lost friend. Pearls have changed the lives of everyone I know. And I have felt my own connection with pearls deepen as they opened me to their secret wonders. Gradually I have come to realize that, while I thought I was working in the pearl business, in fact I have been an adept-in-training at the "Temple of the Pearl."

As we journey together along the Path of the Pearl, I will share the insights and discoveries that working closely with pearls has taught me. We will closely examine the six measures used to evaluate pearls and apply them to our own life review. The path will lead us past the lagoon of the mermaid, our wisdom guide, who will take us on a magical encounter beneath the sea, and gentle healing techniques, poems, and glimmering gems of wisdom will be scattered along our path.

To use this wisdom to learn more of your own inner secrets, I have provided questions at the end of each chapter. I suggest you answer each, either internally or, better still, in a journal. Don't edit your thoughts—just let them come out. In this way you'll be able to appreciate former challenges and to identify the new ones that continue to form the pearls of your life's journey. Whether you choose to meditate or to write, in each new chapter consider the questions that will follow these three themes:

- **Nucleus.** Seminal issues, irritations, or concerns of your life—the very essence of the challenges that have shaped and molded you and the core beliefs around which you have built your life.
- **Layering.** Ways in which you have learned to respond to those basic adversities, irritants, or challenges.
- **Awareness and Beauty.** What you have created from life's irritants—the gifts that have come to you, triggered by the challenges you have faced and your search for self-understanding and self-knowledge.

What can the pearl teach us? As we gaze into her crystal ball, she offers the secrets of the universe, layer by layer, slowly, patiently, a little at a time. Gem of the sea, ocean's gift, torn from a mermaid's necklace, where will you guide us? What mysteries will we learn? What secrets will you whisper to us?

THE PEARL OYSTER

The pearl is the oldest gem, and historically it was considered the most valuable. The chance of a particle of sand, a small crab, or a piece of seaweed or shell naturally drifting into the oyster's body and becoming lodged to create a pearl is literally one in tens of thousands.

A pearl is formed when the pearl-producing oyster defends its soft interior organs against the invasion of a foreign material. At first, the oyster attempts to expel the offender. If the oyster can't reject the foreign object, it will become the nucleus, or center, of the pearl, and the oyster will secrete layers of a protective pearly substance called nacre (NAY-ker) around the irritant to smooth it out.

Fine layers of nacre are applied every second, every minute, and every hour of the day. Some oysters are dormant for part of the year when the water temperature becomes too cold, and others, especially those in the warm waters near the equator, are active all year long.

As the oyster layers the nucleus, it actually transforms the foreign particle into a part of itself. It accepts the intruder, embraces it, and changes it. The oyster uses all the creative forces that are within its realm to overcome the irritant lodged in its body and transform it into a work of nature's art.

Beauty from Adversity

> All art is autobiographical.
> The pearl is the oyster's autobiography.
> — *Federico Fellini*

*T*his miraculous living gift from the sea—the only gemstone to be produced by a living entity— is the creation of beauty from adversity, of art from irritation. It illustrates that even the worst and most painful invasion can become something of healing artistry. The pearl is a glowing example of a mortal threat transformed into magnificence.

As human beings, we know pain and suffering in wondrous variety. We all experience adversity and irritation, loss and anguish. We may encounter failure, death, divorce, and disease. But like the oyster, we can learn to recognize and embrace the transformational opportunities these experiences present.

The oyster coats the surface of an irritant with layer upon layer of pearly nacre, each layer microscopically thin.

These layers are applied in sections and overlap each other like the leaves of a cabbage. The edges of the leaves are jagged, yet this application is so fine that one's fingers feel only a satiny smoothness, and the eye cannot perceive the rough edges.

The memories of our lives are layered like the nacre of a pearl, the petals of a flower, the rings of a tree. These overlapping layers contain the knowledge and learning of each experience. They shape and form us. They smooth the jagged edges of our difficult times. In this way, the nucleus of our pain begins to integrate with the rest of our selves. The irritant journeys a little deeper inside us but becomes less painful.

Like the pearl, our splendor is formed of life's obstacles. The experiences of our lives, both thrilling and challenging, surround the core of our being. It isn't always easy to find the positive in the hardships we endure, but in time, beauty is often revealed. Each challenge is our nucleus for creation, each victorious work of art another pearl on our path. Transformation occurs again and again in our growing process. Every incident, every emotion, every success, every sorrow, becomes another layer of our development. Our pain, which can be unspeakably intense and sometimes debilitating, brings the lessons we never forget. Imprinted deeply in our core, these lessons help us to better weather future provocations.

Like the pearl, a solitary creation in the body of an oyster, the soul's journey and the spirit's adventure is individual; we are essentially alone as we grow in richness and wisdom. As we grow older, wiser, and more able to look with insight at the adversities of our lives, the universe offers up new and deeper levels of learning. Sometimes we find ourselves confronting an old wound we thought had already been healed. But when it reappears, we can see it from a new angle, which allows us to realize a more profound lesson. The pain may become less, and yet the awareness can become even more complete. I've come to firmly believe that none of us will be dealt pain any larger than we can handle. If the adversities seem huge, it is because God or the universe has decided that we are now able to deal with lessons of a much larger magnitude.

The pearl is a glowing reminder that we can make adversity into part of ourselves. Layering iridescent experiences upon the colorful challenges of our life, we culture our soul. As we become aware of the many ways to respond to pain and hardship, we note that some paths are more difficult than others. Some people fixate on the pain, keeping it fresh in their minds for months, years, even decades. Others take small irritations and blow them way out of proportion, making them larger irritations. Complaining about ordeals endured will result in a life overshadowed by unending dissatisfaction. But when we integrate what we have learned from the challenges we have overcome, we can then celebrate them as blessings and further grow and evolve. When we have enough distance, we may ask, "What is there to take away from all of this?" And we discover ways in which the irritant reveals an opening into new arenas of knowledge. We use the lessons learned from each obstacle to become deeper and wiser human beings. These events then become the building blocks of an ever more satisfying life's journey.

How many of us are able to take a challenge, as oysters do, and find the gift in it—to actually turn it into something positive? This is what the pearl teaches us—to honor our strength and flexibility, to find our own beauty in the inner power it takes to bounce back rather than break apart. We surround irritations with a flow of blessings—a spiritual nacre—and we then use those experiences to create pearls.

The Pearly Path

The path of our lives stretches out ahead of us. The Tao, the Way, faith, dharma, the adventure—many words have been used to describe this embarkation into the unknown. We prepare as best we can, drawing on experiences from childhood, what we've learned in school, and other life experiences that have helped us develop our personal code of ethics and morals. We make choices along the way about where to live, who to be friends with, who to fall in love with, whether to marry or have children. We make career choices to help us achieve success in the world. And through the twists and turns of the journey, our path leads us in and out of danger, in and out of sunlight and joy. Along the way we learn many things, and teachers and guides appear to help us along. Sometimes the path forks, and for a while we take a more painful route—one that might have appeared easier but that holds even more opportunities to learn. We follow the path unfailingly through our lives to the mystery beyond.

The path is strewn with the gems and pearls of our lives, loves, joys, successes, and achievements, and it is also littered with the debris of our broken dreams and broken hearts. But even those broken dreams may hold alluring beauty, for all of life is wondrous and magical, containing secrets and hidden wisdom. All of life is an opportunity to learn. The hardest times bring the most profound lessons; the biggest irritants can form the largest pearls. That is the way life instructs us and changes us. If we remain open to the experience and open our hearts and minds to learn from life's hardships, it is then possible to see challenge itself as a precious gift, a treasure—a pearl.

Meditation

I hold a lone pearl in my hand. I gaze upon it to see if I can discern the layers that make its glow so captivating. As I gaze, I discover the layers of its creation.

The pearl is small; it could be lost in a moment of clumsiness. I see the beauty of the little pearl in my hand. I appreciate its delicate fragile essence. But do I see the beauty in myself? Perhaps I am acting more like the crusty oyster, closing my shell around my soft interior, clamping shut to keep out the world. Have I grown a tough shell? Is there an outer wall around the part of me that is soft and

shiny—the pearl of my soul? If so, can I risk opening? Can I let in the world, the ocean, sunlight,
and love? Can I share with others the secret beauty
I hide inside the depths of my being?

COLORS OF PARADISE
There are things that take place
In cool turquoise waters
In languid lagoons, in lovers' hearts.

Exotic secrets shared
Between iridescent shells
Hiding translucent layers born of beauty.

Take a dip at sunrise
In peacock blue waters
Sparkling coral atoll
You have crossed into your dream.

Rest in serene waters
Let your mind breathe
In the mythic land
Of the Rainbow God.

Where bridges of color
Unite with the sea
In a blaze of light.

Giving birth to perfection
Born of ecstatic irritation
She transforms adversity to art.

PEARLS OF WISDOM: The world is what you think it is.
Pain and suffering, or art and beauty? How do you choose to
see the challenges in your life?

Our thoughts, beliefs, and attitudes determine the
results of those tests we face every day. We may not control
the events of our lives, but we have power over the way we
perceive them—and how we respond to them as well. If you
want to see the irritant as something that ruins your life, it
will be so. If you see it as a seed for the creation of something new and beautiful, that is what you will manifest.

When change happens, there are only two possible
responses: acceptance or resistance. But does resistance
ever make circumstances go back to the way they were?
Does resistance ever make anything better? Let challenges
be the seeds of the exquisite pearls of your life.

FURTHER REFLECTION

Nucleus

🐚 What irritant have you experienced that you were later surprised to find you had learned from?

Layering

🐚 How did you first respond to that irritation? Did you hold a grudge? Were you filled with resentment and anger?

🐚 What allowed you to move forward and create the layers that made the experience less difficult?

Awareness and Beauty

🐚 What insight do you have that you wouldn't have gained, if not for a difficult experience?

🐚 How has that lesson had an impact on other parts of your life?

🐚 Did you learn anything significant and enduring about yourself?

The Pearl Divers

Hundreds of years ago, the oyster beds of the world were knee-deep with layers of wild pearl oysters. Pearling ships would bring divers to the abundant beds, and they would free dive, without breathing equipment. The diver who could hold his breath the longest, and therefore collect the most oysters, was the most sought after by the pearling merchants.

At the turn of the twentieth century, thousands of tons of shells were removed from the oceans. All over the world, the once-plentiful oyster beds have since been virtually wiped out by overfishing.

Today, only pearl farmers may dive for pearls on their underwater farms on remote islands and atolls. Farmers collect baby oysters in the wild and raise them for years, painstakingly caring for them, protecting them from predators, turning them, and scraping barnacles, starfish, and other creatures off the growing shells.

When the oysters reach maturity, the farmer hires a specially trained grafting technician to insert a tiny nucleus made of shell into each oyster's tender body. The grafter seeds the oysters, and they are returned to the water, where they are carefully tended for several more years. They are marked and dated and observed daily by the farmer as he swims between the lines of oysters that are his livelihood.

2

Shape, the Individual

And precious the tear as that rain from the sky,
Which turns into pearls as it falls in the sea.
— *Thomas Moore*

The pearl comes to us in a perfect and alluring form, requiring no polishing or cutting to reveal its beauty. The wide range of pearl shapes is testimony to the lack of control the pearl farmer has in manipulating the oyster to make perfect, round pearls. Though every nucleus inserted into every oyster for cultured marine or saltwater pearls is round, only a small percentage of the world's pearl harvests are perfect, round pearls—the most difficult shape for the oyster to create—and therefore they are the most rare.

The terms usually used to describe the natural shapes are *spherical* (or round), *symmetrical* (tear or pear-shaped), and *baroque* (all other shapes). And there are new shapes arriving on the freshwater pearl market. Shapes such as "potato," "coin," "bar," and "cross" join the more familiar "rice," "seed," and "oblong" shapes.

At the pearl auctions in Tahiti, pearls are categorized as round, semi-round, drop, oval, button, and circle. This breakdown helps the auction organizers separate pearls by basic shape, but in reality there is a much wider variety of shapes within those basic categories. Within each shape are also additional descriptions such as short, long, and extra long.

No two pearls are exactly alike, but each shape is prized and used by master jewelers to create a uniquely beautiful design. The primary consideration in regard to shape is what is right for *you*—not some objective idea of what is *best*. We find that many women are drawn to baroque pearls, enchanted by their irregular shapes. "Oh, I love this! It's so different!" they say.

Humans, too, are not perfectly symmetrical. Life shapes us. Like a sculptor working and molding clay, hammering and polishing metal, or carving and sanding wood, every experience, success, or failure creates the contours of our being. We participate in this shaping as well. Our decisions and choices create the twists and turns in our life's journey. Genetic influences also define part of the basic template of who we are, what shape we will grow to be. In broad hips or small feet, we carry proud physical distinctions inherited from our mothers and grandmothers.

More than any other attribute, the concept of shape seems to plague many women. We worry that we may not fit the current concept of beauty. What shape is the right one? One person may be tall with long slender legs and a tendency to be chubby; another may be small-boned with a very long waist and neck; while another may be wider than she is tall.

We, too, are uniquely beautiful creations, each with our own distinctive qualities. We are one-of-a-kind, rare treasures, worthy of being sought-after and cherished. This message of the pearl is self-acceptance and self-love.

Not only do we have a unique shape, but we are also shape-shifters. At each stage of our lives we find that our shape is ever-changing. Our bodies can stretch and transform dramatically. We have all changed shape many times as we have grown up. From a tiny egg to an infant, a toddler, a child, we embodied a new shape and size. Think back to when you first became aware of your body. How old were you? Then see yourself at ten, fifteen, eighteen, twenty-five, thirty-five, forty-five.

Have you ever looked back and realized you actually looked much better than you let yourself feel at the time? Imagine if you had just let yourself enjoy that shape and that body; think how much happier you would have been. What makes it so difficult for us to accept and love ourselves? Why are we often driven to strive for a shape that bears no connection to our genetic makeup? Women's body shapes vary at least as much as pearl shapes, and yet we are bombarded with messages telling us we should all be the same—or at least feel guilty and diminished if we do not.

In reality, we could all be categorized as baroque-shaped. Baroque is a wonderful word in pearl terminology. It means "anything that is not round." As very few pearls are perfectly round, all other pearl shapes, large or small, whether oval, drop, beehive, mushroom, irregular, or circle, are defined as baroque. And just like baroque pearls, we are to be cherished for our individuality and all considered valuable. Nature has made us in the incredibly diverse shapes we are—not carbon copies of one body type.

What is special about you? What can you say about yourself, or what have you heard others say about you, that sets you apart? It could be time to take a good look. In ancient times, only a queen could afford a treasure like a mirror. Most people didn't know what they looked like, unless they saw themselves in a still body of water. Only the wealthy had the power to look at themselves—to really look.

The mirror is a powerful ally. It clearly discerns every strength and asset. However, it also shows every shadow and line, every dark mood, every blemish. Have you ever tried to stand nude in front of the mirror for more than a few seconds? It can be hard, because your mind might choose to focus on the things you don't like about your body, face, or hair. But if you stay with it, just sitting quietly and letting thoughts float away, you give yourself the gift of true attention. Look at the softness and the contours of your unique shape and feel your breath—the connection between the life force and your physical body. Allow yourself to be grateful for your body. Be thankful that you live, breathe, and move.

The pearl invites you to stretch the boundaries of your shape, to love yourself in any form, to embrace the changes over time, to know that change is growth. It invites you to take charge of changes in your shape, molding your body by eating well, spending time with friends who energize you, and getting both rest and exercise. It invites you to gently accept the changes bestowed through time and experience, feeling your wisdom grow as you learn to appreciate your body in all its forms. We can give thanks for the gift of shape and accept our body in its current form.

The Blessing of Self-Acceptance

As women, we often subject ourselves and our bodies to the harshest scrutiny. No matter what the scale reads, what the dress-size label says, too often we feel too big, too fat, occasionally too thin, but too often simply the wrong shape. You can choose to make a pact with yourself right now to end this self-imposed torture. Conduct an inner inventory of your qualities and remind yourself that you are a beautiful, good, and deserving person. Bless the parts of yourself that you admire and appreciate. If you were to see these qualities in another woman, you would feel that she should take pride in them. Give yourself the same appreciation and acknowledgment that you so naturally give to others.

Here is a list I have developed in my own journey toward self-acceptance and self-love. See if these qualities of self-acceptance and self-love resonate for you.

- To forgive self and others; to release; to let the past go
- To gracefully honor one's talents
- To tenderly care for oneself

- ❧ To eat healthfully
- ❧ To choose friends well; to surround oneself with positive people
- ❧ To balance sleep, rest, exercise, and joy of body and movement
- ❧ To resolve family conflicts; to maintain healthy, loving relationships
- ❧ To learn from everything; to perceive challenges as gifts; to embrace change as growth
- ❧ To strive for excellence; to give back generously
- ❧ To keep a calm center; to honor spiritual interests; to bless self and others; to pray, reflect, and heal

Whenever you feel yourself starting to think judgmental or critical thoughts about yourself, please remember these seven statements of self-appreciation:

- ❧ I know who I am and where I am in my life, and I feel gratitude for all the blessings I have received.
- ❧ I release all fears, unhappiness, and doubts, knowing that my needs will always be provided for.
- ❧ I focus on exactly what I want, knowing that I direct my own experiences.

🐚 I feel the power of the moment, remembering that nothing in the past or future is as important as now.

🐚 I love myself and my purpose, knowing that only I can make my unique contribution to the world.

🐚 I trust my spirit and the world, knowing that my instincts will guide me and the world will care for me.

🐚 I do whatever is appropriate and effective, using the wisdom I have gathered over the course of my life.

Repeat these statements whenever your confidence needs a boost.

APHRODITE'S TEMPLE

I swim along the bottom of the ocean.

Large white boulders are strewn across the ocean floor and broken columns lie on their sides. A vast marble building is in the distance; I swim closer and recognize it as a huge temple. The temple is in decline and disrepair. Its stately columns are broken, the roof has slid to one side, and the steps have crumbled.

Swimming alongside its majestic walls, I find the grand entry and see tall white marble columns supporting the towering carved ceiling that looms overhead. I enter another even more impressive inner hallway, and there, in the middle of the room, stands an enormous statue. The statue is female, and it is strewn with sand, moss, barnacles, and rocks and draped in unruly garments of seaweed and kelp.

I swim over and begin to unwrap huge pieces of kelp that have fallen around and over those stone shoulders. I remove more and more seaweed, revealing the intricate carved folds of her gown and the smooth magnificence of her carved marble exterior. I run my hand along her shoulder and arm, feeling the sensuous curve of her elbow, the line of her neck.

"She is so lovely," I think.

"She has forgotten her beauty so completely," says a voice.

"How sad," I say aloud.

I search for the source of that voice and then realize that its source is not important.

Suddenly, I weep. Deep in the ocean of salt water, I weep tears of salt water. My weeping becomes the sea, and my tears are the ocean, the

ocean my tears. I feel loss and sadness. My despair
is as great as the world.

The voice sings a sweet lullaby, a soft caress
that fills me with such love and kindness I feel
light-headed.

"This temple is your temple of love, your inner
and outer beauty," the voice says. As she speaks, I
feel another wave of sadness and grief.

"Why haven't I seen how beautiful I am? Why
have I only nourished others and not fed myself?"
I ask aloud. "Why does my love of myself mean so
little to me?"

I remove the last of the seaweed and kelp from
that smooth white marble and gaze up at this
marvelous symbol of feminine beauty and love.
Aphrodite stands before me, smiling with understanding and graceful acceptance.

I look into her eyes and suddenly I'm trans-
ported to an ancient land. The temple stands atop a
hill, gleaming white in the sunlight. Thousands of
people stand in line to enter its doors to worship
the goddess. They hold baskets of fruit; they carry
goats and lambs; they balance jugs of honey on

their heads as well as bolts of cloth. They smile in anticipation of praying to the goddess.

Inside the temple are lovely priestesses, chosen for their elegance and grace, who spend their lives serving the goddess, singing and dancing to her glory. They greet the devotees and usher them inside, several at a time. I join a group of these worshippers. As I enter the temple, I gasp as she comes into view. She is Aphrodite, the goddess of human and divine love, of pleasure and beauty, of femininity and sensuality. I fall to my knees along with the others, and I set my gifts on the ground before her. I hear the muttered prayers of the supplicants.

"Oh goddess, please bring me children so I may have a family with my beloved husband," asks one young bride.

"Goddess, give me the man I love. Make him love me in return."

"Goddess, help me find my soul mate so with him may I find love."

"Goddess, grant me loveliness and kindness so I may bring pleasure to my lover." The voices of the worshippers grow in number and volume around me.

What do I want? I find myself wondering. Finally the answer comes to me.

"Goddess," I say, "remind me to honor myself, to care for myself. Help me celebrate, not belittle, my beauty. Help me appreciate the attributes I have rather than focusing on those I do not."

As I speak these words to the goddess, I feel lighter and happier than I have felt as long as I can remember. The weight of self-condemnation lifts from me; the pain of complaining, comparing, and blaming eases and drifts away.

I realize that I am responsible for nourishing my inner beauty, this sacred part of myself, and that no one can do it for me. I can do it only by caring for and cleaning the temple of self-love, only by rigorously removing the debris of self-loathing and denial. To accept myself, to honor myself, and to truly *love* myself will be the building blocks of my confidence and self-esteem. To believe in myself means that all self-abusive activities must end. Rather than sending messages of doubt to myself, my inner messages must now be loving and healing.

I look back at the temple one last time and vow to return here often. I know the temple of love and beauty is my sanctuary, and I know I will never forget it again.

I swim up toward the light.

PEARLS OF WISDOM: To love is to be happy with yourself. To accept yourself, to be happy with things, to feel no need to change or fix anything, is the ultimate state of peace.

It is time to be kind to yourself. Set yourself free from the tyranny of self-judgment, free to enjoy your perfect baroque, "anything that is not round" physical manifestation, without pressure, without resistance, without fears and self-doubts.

We are shape-shifters, adapting to life's changes. Flexible and strong like bamboo, we bend rather than break. Like a pearl cherished for its unique shape, we celebrate our individuality. And we love ourselves.

FURTHER REFLECTION

Nucleus

Do you balance your attention to your physical appearance with your attention to your inner qualities?

❀ Do you judge yourself now based on an earlier self-image you still hold in your mind?

❀ Do you measure your appearance against an unrealistic ideal?

Layering

❀ What have you done to help yourself appreciate your positive qualities, physical and otherwise, in the same way that you appreciate those qualities in others?

❀ Have you developed a strategy to boost your confidence when you need it? Could you perhaps focus on the parts of yourself you always feel good about?

Awareness and Beauty

❀ Do you remember to demonstrate your self-love? How can you reward yourself? What will make you feel special—a facial, a massage, a pedicure, an art class, a shopping spree?

Mother-of-Pearl

The term mother-of-pearl refers to the iridescent, pearly inside shell of the oyster. All pearl-producing species of mollusks have a lining that can "mother" pearls.

The mother oyster does not have to be killed to remove the pearl. If the newly harvested pearl is considered of good quality, the oyster will immediately be seeded with a new nucleus and returned to the lagoons to grow a new pearl. If the pearl is not good, the oyster is still returned to the lagoon to replenish the natural oyster beds.

Before the age of plastics, most of the buttons for the clothing of the Western world depended on the lucrative business of fishing for mother-of-pearl. Oyster shells were raised out of the ocean and stacked on the decks of pearling ships, the shells were opened and cleaned, and the meat was discarded. If a pearl was found during the cleaning process, it was an extra benefit, but the primary goal was to obtain the shells.

Used in ancient times as money, today mother-of-pearl is used in a variety of costume-jewelry pieces and other decorative gifts. Fishermen in the South Pacific use the iridescent shell for fishing lures. It is also inlayed in wood furniture, Japanese lacquer boxes, and musical instruments such as guitars and mandolins.

3

Size, Room for Expansion

I firmly believe that the universe dreams a much bigger
dream for you than you can dream for yourself.
— *Oprah Winfrey*

*I*n 1560, a slave diving off the
coast of Panama found a pearl so huge and rare it was named
La Pelegrina, which means "The Incomparable." A pear-
shaped pearl, La Pelegrina was noted for its astounding
beauty.

The slave was granted his freedom, the slave's master
was made the mayor of the town, and the pearl traveled to
Spain and into the possession of King Philip II. From there,
La Pelegrina traveled into the jewel collections of various
monarchs including Napoleon III and Mary Tudor, daugh-
ter of Henry VIII of England, and eventually it came into the
possession of a wealthy English family.

In 1969 it was purchased for only $37,000 by Richard
Burton, who presented it to his wife, Elizabeth Taylor. It is

27.88 carats and about the size of a pigeon's egg—one of the largest and most valuable natural pearls ever found.

The size of a pearl is affected by the species of pearl-producing oyster, the size and health of the oyster, the nucleus, and the thickness of the multiple layers of nacreous pearl material secreted around the nucleus. Depending on the type of oyster, pearls can be as small as a tiny bead or as large as a bird's egg.

Large pearls are the stuff of dreams, generating much press and public excitement when discovered. But those of us who work with pearls know that biggest doesn't necessarily mean best. When someone selects a pearl, the ideal size is the one that best complements its setting and the wearer. No pearl is the "perfect" size; it is a matter of personal preference.

Wouldn't it be nice if we applied that same standard of measuring value to our lives? What *is* the perfect size for a house? Car? Career? Family? If size is a matter of personal preference, then there's a different "right" size for everyone.

As discussed in the previous chapter, our physical bodies deserve to be accepted and valued regardless of shape or size. To achieve this, we strive to recognize our inherent qualities, those universally enjoyed as the birthright of every human being. Similarly, when we evaluate ourselves, size plays an important role only when we look at our inherent inner qualities. The size of your spirit and your capacity for such values as love and generosity, honesty and faith, integrity and devotion are far more significant than physical appearance and will have a greater impact on the world and others around you.

What is the size of our capacity for acceptance and love? Expansion in this area will bring us nothing but joy! The size of our love, for others and for ourselves, is the ultimate use of this criterion for evaluation. Have you measured your capacity for giving and—just as important—receiving love? Some people seem to have such an abundance to share with the world. They are loving to all they meet, they lavish love and attention on their families, and they have the capacity to inspire and accept huge amounts of love in return.

Are you generous with others? Do you give freely to family, lovers, and friends? Are you generous with your smile, with a kind word, with your thoughtfulness? And most importantly, do you generously love yourself? Do you remember to balance your care of others with attention to your own needs? Do you allow others to lavish love on you as well?

Dream Your Dreams

Throughout history, magical powers and even healing properties have been attributed to the pearl, which is possibly the reason that pearls of unusual size capture the public's imagination as they do. They are symbols of potency and potential, of magic often only dreamed of. And like dreams, the promise they hold is immense and unlimited, unfettered by constraints of physical reality. Here the pearl reminds us: There are no limits. The possibilities of what we can do, of what is possible to experience, are endless. We have the potential to realize far bigger dreams than we think.

Ironically, we are socialized to endlessly reach within innately constricting environments dependent on definitions, labels, and expectations. Caught up in this tide, we often find ourselves too busy dealing with our daily lives to remember the dreams we had as children. But there comes a time as we get older when some of us find the time to reconnect with our dreams, to live life fully, to make a difference, to do what we came here to do. It's never too late to live up to our potential, to dream big dreams, and to make those dreams come true. Let go of those limitations you have come to accept; let go of the expectations you have developed or have had dictated to you. Your dreams can be boundless, just as the line of the horizon is without end.

THE SEA GODDESS

My cabinets are oyster shells,
In which I keep my orient pearls;
To open them I use the tide,
As keys to locks, which opens wide
The oyster shells, then out I take
Those orient pearls and crowns do make;
And modest coral do I wear,
Which blushes when it touches air.
On silver waves I sit and sing,
And then the fish lie listening;
Then sitting on a rocky stone
I comb my hair with fishes' bone;
The whilst Apollo with his beams
Doth dry my hair from watery streams.
His light doth glaze the waters' face,
Make the large sea my looking-glass:
So when I swim on waters high,
I see myself as I glide by:
But when the sun begins to burn,

I back into my waters turn,
And dive unto the bottom low:
Then on my head the waters flow
In curled waves and circles round,
And thus with waters am I crowned.

—Margaret Cavendish, Duchess of Newcastle (1624–74)

PEARLS OF WISDOM: **The smaller vessel more easily overflows.**

In a tiny oyster, a small pearl will still look big. Put the same pearl in a larger oyster, and it will appear to shrink. This also happens with our lives. When we look at all the material things available in the wide world, our pearl may seem small. Yet if we remember the things we *really* need—warmth, comfort, love, food—we may better appreciate how rich we truly are. If we take the time to appreciate and be grateful for all we have, our modest oyster will barely be able to contain its treasure. By setting sights on wanting more and more—the bigger house, the fancier car—the oyster grows so big it can never be full, and therefore, the pearl will always be inadequate.

This is not to say that we need limit our expectations for our lives but rather that we should give better attention to all the wonders we enjoy every day, without over-looking, dismissing, or taking for granted. We live in a world where some people still have no running water or electric light, where there isn't enough food, medicine, or love. Take time to notice and give thanks for all you have and your bliss will grow.

FURTHER REFLECTION

Nucleus

🐚 Was there ever a time in your life when you felt so insecure that you lost sight of the importance of loving and giving to others?

🐚 Have you ever withheld love from yourself? Did something suddenly make you notice that you were needlessly punishing yourself?

Layering

🐚 Focus not on your physical size but on the size of your hopes, dreams, and goals. How big is your vision for your life?

🐚 How large is your passion for living and giving? How do others benefit from the capacity of your loving generosity?

Awareness and Beauty

 How big is your inner self?

 What are some examples in your life of important things—and important people—that may have been either very small or very large? How significant was their size?

BLACK PEARLS

"*Black*" is in fact a misnomer. Tahitian pearls are not all black. In fact, they come in a glorious range of colors, including but not limited to light gray, silver, aqua, pink, lavender, sea green, forest green, iridescent peacock green, eggplant, magenta, purple, peach, canary, gold, bronze, copper, root beer, teal, baby blue, navy, indigo, smoke, platinum, dark gray, gunmetal, twilight black, and midnight black.

They came to be called black pearls because the parent oyster, known as the "black-lipped" oyster, has a black lip rimming the edges of its shell. The black lip is called the mantle, the part of the creature responsible for creating the multitude of rainbow colors in pearls.

This huge oyster can live for thirty years and grow to the size of a turkey platter. The crusty exterior of the oyster's shell blends in with the surrounding rocks and coral reef where it attaches itself to grow. Oysters live on plankton, just as whales do, opening and closing their shells to filter thousands of gallons of water in order to eat.

4

The Dance of Color

The pearls that long have slept,
These were tears by Naiads wept.
— *Sir Walter Scott*

*I*n ancient times it was thought that pearls were created from dew and that white pearls were formed in fair weather and dark pearls during storms. According to South Seas legend, Tahitian black pearls were created from a marriage of moonlight and rainbow when the god Oro descended from the sky along a rainbow bridge and bits of rainbow color washed into the sea. Shimmering, iridescent, and exotic, black pearls were cherished by Tahitian royalty as gifts of the gods. They were thought to be the ultimate symbol of love and romance, good-luck talismans for both giver and receiver.

When evaluating pearls, color is divided into two categories: body color and overtone. Body color is the most obvious or basic color. Those most often seen are white, cream, gold, gray, and black. It is the body color that gives the background, and it is a rich canvas for the overtones. These secondary colors—the overtones of iridescent hues— are those that appear to be on top of the basic color. Pearl color is the combination, or interplay, of both the body color and the overtones. No other attribute delights our senses as much as color, and some pearls have as many as seven or eight vibrant colors. Each pearl is unique, each color combination different—intense radiant colors, opalescent and iridescent, shimmering with richness and depth. They are mesmerizing and irresistible.

Pearl color is determined by the conchiolin in the nacre. The various tints and shades may have to do with the health of the oyster, the water temperature, the nutrients and chemi-cals in the water, the salinity of the water, or the DNA of the mother oyster. In fact, all of these factors probably play a part in the colors of pearl nacre the oyster produces, but there is no exact scientific explanation for pearl color. And as with shape and size, color is impossible for the pearl farmer to control. Though man assists with the introduction of the nucleus, no one but the pearl oyster and the forces of nature controls the palette of colors. Each color is an act of artistry, luck, and magic. It is the ultimate expression of creativity.

For us, color represents creativity, diversity, artistry, and flair. Colors can be used to symbolize personality, character, and style. Through the joy of expressing oneself, we take advantage of life's rainbow of possibilities and discover the interplay of darkness and light, the seen and the unseen. We are surrounded by a bounty of sensory delights that are saturated with color. Swirling around us, organized into shapes and objects, these colors delight and inspire.

Color and creativity are precious gifts. We might be tickled by the bright lavender of a car's custom paint job, the pulsing red of a woman's shoe, the brilliant green of a newly formed leaf. Vivid patterns of colors, textures, contours, and lines dazzle our eyes. What generosity created this abundance for our pleasure? Blessed as we are with the joy of color and the spirit of creativity in every moment of our lives, creativity offers our most direct access to the Divine. To sit quietly, to relax and open one's heart and mind, to let go all thoughts and just be—from that space comes true connection with spirit and great inspiration. The little talent unites with the Big Talent, and from there creation begins to blossom, ideas and phrases flow onto the page in a gleeful dance.

We are all artists with unlimited choices of ways to present our creativity to the world. By writing, painting, singing, dancing, cooking, decorating our homes, or stylishly adorning ourselves as pieces of walking, living art, we demonstrate infinite variety in the ways we can make our lives more colorful.

Creative energy is one of the most abiding characteristics universally shared by cultures since time immemorial. Clearly, the wish to give expression to our deepest emotions and feelings so we may share them with others is one of our most basic human desires. Some of us are blessed to fulfill this desire more easily than others. I am fortunate, for example, to have come from a highly creative family. My grandmother was a talented painter, and she loved collecting beach glass, arranging flowers, and sewing all the clothes for herself and her two daughters. My mother is exceptionally talented and fascinated by all types of creative self-expression. When I was growing up, our home was her art and sewing studio, with projects spread out on every surface. She taught us to sew and drove us to countless dance lessons, choir practices, language classes, and piano lessons.

Like so many women of her generation, my mother dedicated herself to her children, living many of her own artistic and professional ambitions through us. She celebrated all forms of creative curiosity, encouraging us to perform puppet shows, dance events, and street pageants for the neighborhood. It was a glorious way to grow up, and I can never thank her enough for her inspiration and joyful acknowledgment of our creations.

For those of us who don't come from such encouraging environments or who haven't been driven by an irresistible inner call, it can sometimes be difficult to get started, either from fear of criticism or simply from being overwhelmed by uncertainty about how to begin. As we all know, the art world—particularly the fine arts—can be an exclusive, intimidating environment. If you find yourself wishing to express yourself creatively but unable to do it by yourself, I recommend finding a supportive, encouraging group to help. Community colleges and art centers offer classes, and creative-writing programs will usually provide information about writing groups—or you could even form one yourself, enrolling friends, neighbors, or colleagues with similar aspirations.

It takes courage, but by digging deep and heeding the call you have so long heard inside, you will open yourself up to immense, inexhaustible satisfaction—and growth. It is the creative process, not the end result, that will continue to delight and sustain you.

The type of creative medium to explore is your individual choice—just as personal preference is the most important factor in selecting pearl color. Different pearl colors come alive on different people, depending on eye color, hair color, skin tone. A dark green pearl might be gorgeous on one person, while her best friend looks smashing wearing a silver-pink pearl. As you try one after another, a special color will attract your attention. Enjoy the entire rainbow of pearl colors. They blend in a symphony of beauty.

Everyone has innate talent, and sometimes we must try on different "colors" to find the best outlets for this energy. One person may be a painter; another may excel at sports. Some may know the path they will follow from childhood; others may search for their true colors over a lifetime. Not only will different people try to express themselves in different ways, but these ways will often change over time. Whether you master an art or begin to tire of it, remember that the source of inspiration is boundless, that you can always freshly reconnect with the divine and give voice to it in some new way.

This connection to the divine also connects us to each other. When we witness the art of others, our own inner creative spark flares higher and we feel connected to the artist who inspired the emotional response with their own creative energy. Our spark grows to a flame that unites us to every other human being. As the flame burns brighter, in a circular manner we are once more closely connected with our Source, the ultimate Creative Force.

PEARLS OF WISDOM: You have choices.
You have a rainbow of choices, and the choices you make now along the path are what will determine the trajectory you follow.

Why not walk this path of life with as much color, creativity, personality, and fun as possible? Life is not drudgery—life is a dance! Everything in our lives, everything on earth, everything we encounter is just part of its intricate choreography. It is all here for our learning and for our pleasure.

Our creative self-expression, like the iridescent colors of a pearl, brings rainbows of joy into the dance of our lives. It's all up to you—you are the dancer. Why not choose enjoyment as a goal?

FURTHER REFLECTION

Nucleus

🐚 Have you ever used a personal experience as the starting place for creative expression, such as a painting or piece of writing?

Layering

🐚 Where was your creativity born? Did someone in your family influence you through his or her particular talents or encourage you to develop yours?

🐚 Is there a creative field you have always been attracted to but never dared to try? Acting? Singing? Photography? Can you find an encouraging outlet for that energy?

Awareness and Beauty

🐚 If life is a dance, what are you dancing? A tango? A waltz?

🐚 Which colors make you feel beautiful, strong, powerful, intelligent, or happy? How do you respond to color in art?

NATURAL OR CULTURED?

Pearls are either natural or cultured. "Natural" pearls are those that occur in the wild. Natural pearls are rarely round; they are generally slightly baroque in shape. Collectors will pay enormous sums for these incredibly rare gems, which have not been found in any quantity for hundreds of years. The governments of the pearl-producing countries have banned diving for pearls in the wild in order to protect the natural oyster beds.

When a pearl is "cultured," it means the oyster was assisted in the earliest phase of pearl creation. A grafter places a small round bead made from the shell of a Mississippi Pig Toe mussel into the oyster along with a small piece of the mantle tissue from a donor oyster to stimulate the production of nacre.

For some unknown reason, the Pig Toe mussel's shell is most easily embraced by oysters of all varieties, and the rate of rejection is considerably lower than any other artificial nucleus. Pearl producers the world over use this same mussel shell. The Japanese have tried plastic, glass, and numerous other shells, yet still they must buy their nucleus material from the United States.

In every other way, natural and cultured pearls are the same. Today, all pearls marketed in the jewelry venues of the world are cultured.

5

Luster, Shimmering Mirror

Gleaming like polished silver,
the pearl reflects another doorway to the soul.

Luster, one of the most
important of the six criteria for determining a pearl's quality, is a smooth sheen, a clear reflection like a perfect
mirror. This surface shine depends on the structure of the
skin of the pearl and the quality of the nacre.

Luster is created by thousands of fine layers of nacre
deposited on the pearl's surface as the oyster pulses and
turns. Tiny crystals cause the layers of nacre to reflect light.
Fine-quality nacre has smaller and more transparent crystals, and the finer and smoother the pearl nacre, the higher
the luster. Superior nacre is mostly translucent; the clearest
luster indicates the highest-quality pearls. The fine quality
of the layers as well as the depth of thickness between the
nucleus and the outside skin of the pearl is what most

determines the luster. The thicker the depth of the nacre, the better the luster.

Luster is a study in contrasts—the brightness of the area of the pearl exposed to the most light contrasted with the area of the pearl in shadow. In a pearl with excellent luster, the contrast between this bright and shadow creates the impression of a rounded "ball" shape in the center of the pearl. Imitation pearls and beads often have a shiny surface. This is not luster. Luster is not superficial; it is more of an intense brightness that seems to emanate from within the pearl itself. The luster of a pearl sets off the beauty of the wearer and adds a sparkle and glow to the ears, neck, and fingers. And just as a pearl with excellent luster creates a tiny mirror of the world, our own luster reflects what we think and feel to the world around us.

Like the pearl, our individual luster isn't superficial but rather indicates the quality of the layers of experiences and relationships that shape us over time. Carl Jung wrote, "He who looks in the 'mirror'. . . sees first of all his own image. He who goes toward himself risks meeting himself. The mirror does not flatter; it shows accurately that which is being reflected, that is the face which we never reveal to the world, because we conceal it behind the persona, the actor's mask. . . ."

Imagine looking deeply into a beautiful, high-quality pearl and seeing your own image reflected back. What do you see? The reflections of who we are change constantly, and at times it can be difficult to look directly at ourselves and see beyond the surface; to gain a deeper understanding of the inner self, it can be helpful to look at the world we create for ourselves. For example, in the same way that the sharpness and clarity of the luster reflects the quality of a pearl, to a certain degree our relationships with people around us reveal something about the quality of our lives. The company we keep— friends, family, co-workers—are all mirrors, reflecting who we are to ourselves and others through the relationships we pursue and the way we conduct ourselves within those relationships.

Have you ever noticed a correspondence between someone's outer life and their apparent inner state? Haven't we all had a friend whose inner turmoil is clearly reflected by the chaos all around her, including tumultuous relationships with partners, parents, and children? Then there are those serene people who seem to coexist harmoniously with everyone, who—with apparent ease—always find quick resolutions to problems. It can be helpful to slow down occasionally and take a look at one's surroundings to see if the exterior gives any clue about the interior.

Meditation

Picture yourself standing before a mirror, looking at your reflection—not your physical appearance but your inner self. Are you reflected back clearly? Are any parts obscured? Take out a cloth and work on any parts of the mirror that are cloudy or speckled, touching up areas of your luster that need brightening. Consider where these clouds come from: Are there old grudges or hurts from the past that you have not addressed? What casts a shadow on your mirror's clarity?

It requires courage, but think carefully about your relationships with family and with friends. Are you confronted with anything unfulfilling or destructive? Are you comforted by feelings of encouragement? Are you surrounded by people who are unsupportive, critical, and demeaning? Are you energized by anyone's positive influence?

Think about a particularly challenging relationship and let your mind be open to possible causes

Paradise

pacific-image.com

Let the image of water sustain you. Water is life itself.

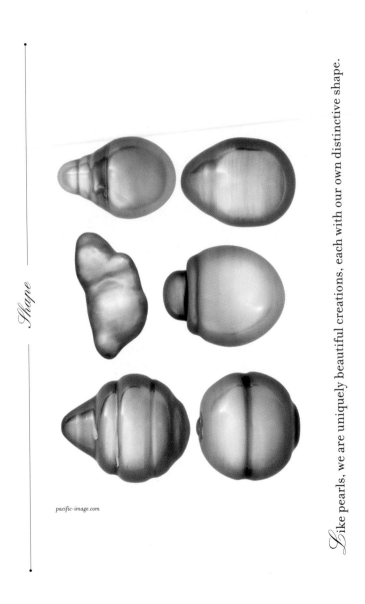

Like pearls, we are uniquely beautiful creations, each with our own distinctive shape.

Size

pacific-image.com

There is no such thing as the perfect size: It's a matter of what is right for you.

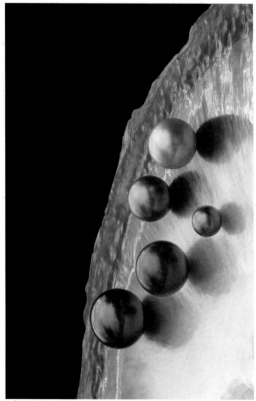

Color and creativity are precious gifts.

Luster

pacific-image.com

*L*uster isn't superficial: It's an intense brightness that emanates from within.

Orient

*L*ooking beneath the surface, we catch a glimpse of our brilliant inner light.

Perfection

pacific-image.com

The identifying marks on the surface are part of what makes us special.

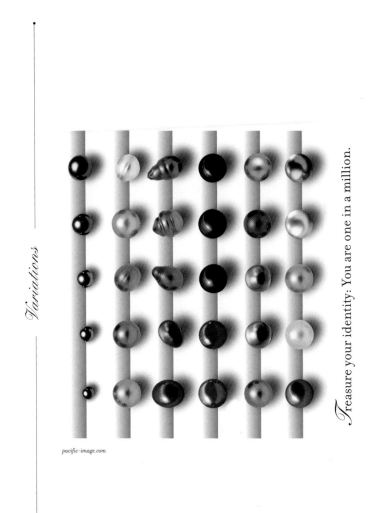

Variations

pacific-image.com

*T*reasure your identity: You are one in a million.

of the problem that you may have never considered. Sometimes we dislike something in someone else because that person reflects our own negative behavior back to us. Or they may display a characteristic that we dislike in ourselves. As you strive to gain deeper insight into the nature of the relationship, also let your mind be open to creative ways to improve it.

Now turn your thoughts to other relationships. Who are your friends? How do they reflect parts of yourself that you love? Do you have friends you no longer enjoy? Do you notice any of your friends having a negative effect on you? Do they not understand your need to grow, or do they try to prevent it in some way? Sometimes direct communication will allow you to reset the course of your life with boundaries your friends can respect if not completely understand. Or sometimes, when looking with clear eyes at a clear reflection of ourselves, we learn to recognize when it is time to move on. Outgrowing friends can be one of the hardest of life's experiences, involving confrontation, breaking away, and moving apart.

But it is vital to surround yourself with people who nurture and love you. Letting go of negative relationships creates space for healthy, loving ones to form. Visualize yourself interacting with people who nurture you and make your luster brighter. Seek out positive people who support you and want you to be happy. And as you do, forgive those who have been difficult in your life. Expect yourself to be treated well.

Once you have looked at all your family and friends, don't forget to take a close look at your relationship with yourself. How are you treating yourself? Does your mirror reflect a happy, healthy person filled with self-love? If not, what can you do to make that your reality?

If you have the courage to look, awareness can help you get clear about what you need to change in your physical and social environments and even in the attitudes you hold. When we turn our full attention to ourselves, it can be hard to accept what we see—at times, we may not even recognize ourselves. The cleaner we keep our mirror, the better it reflects the images of whatever passes before it.

How do we clean our mirror and brighten our luster? Forgiveness is the answer.

PEARLS OF WISDOM: There is no greater power than forgiveness.

Practicing forgiveness can be an excellent way to release old pain and clear the mirror of your life. If you can forgive those who have hurt you, you will set yourself free. If you can forgive yourself, you can reach your greatest potential and make your life into a shining example of the triumph of beauty over adversity, love over fear, happiness over suffering. That is the power of forgiveness.

The dictionary defines *forgive* as "to grant pardon without harboring resentment, to excuse for a fault or offense." Forgiveness is one of the most direct, effective, and powerful healing tools that exists. Total forgiveness means giving up all desire to punish yourself or to punish the other person. And remember: Forgiving someone does not mean you are saying the other person is right!

Letting go of anger from old wounds releases you from a heavy burden. It is a gift to yourself as well as to those you feel have wronged you. Forgive others, and don't forget to forgive yourself. When we dwell on past mistakes we have made or injustices we have suffered, we lose sight of the lessons those experiences are meant to teach us. Inevitably, life throws back the same lessons over and over until we have learned what we need. So look closely at what you have experienced and continue to experience—and let yourself get ready to experience something new.

FURTHER REFLECTION

Nucleus

- What relationships have challenged you in your life? Which have caused you pain?
- Can you think of anyone in your life who reflects parts of yourself you don't care for? Can you find a way to view those attributes (in yourself and in the other person) with respect and compassion?

Layering

- Have you ever worked through a difficult connection with someone and ultimately gained deeper respect for that person or even made friends?
- How have you worked to improve your relationships?
- Which people in your life most define you?

Awareness and Beauty

🐚 What gifts have come to you as a result of your relationships?

🐚 Have painful relationships also had loving elements or helped you grow in some way?

🐚 Friends and associates add luster to our lives. What can you change when you feel your luster is dull?

THE FATHER OF THE CULTURED PEARL

At the turn of the last century, many inventors worked diligently to find a way to stimulate pearl oysters to create pearls, but it is Kokichi Mikimoto who is credited with inventing the process of culturing pearls. Often referred to as the father of Japan's pearl industry, Mikimoto patented the procedure in 1903, and his place in history was secured.

Mikimoto was also a dynamic marketing genius. Historically, pearls had been worn only by royalty and the extremely wealthy. Suddenly, it was possible for every woman to afford a strand of pearls. Once, as a promotional stunt, Mikimoto bulldozed a mountain of what he considered to be subquality pearls, smashing them to dust and making the point that he would sell only the finest-quality cultured pearls.

Smitten by pearls and always good at attracting publicity, Mikimoto stated, "I owe my ninety-four years of long, healthy life to the two pearls I have swallowed every morning since I was twenty."

6

Orient, Soul of the Pearl

Aphrodite's worshippers called her
the Pearl of the Sea.

$\mathcal{T}$he orient of the pearl is the glow from within, the iridescence or hue, sometimes called the "soul." Difficult to observe by the untrained eye, orient is the subtlest of the six major pearl-grading criteria. Rather than reflecting from the surface of the pearl as fine luster does, orient is defined as the way the light refracts deeply within the pearl nacre. The nacre must be unusually thick to support the prism effect of white light dividing into all the colors of the rainbow. Pearls with high orient have a unique crystalline form, each pearly coating comprising thousands of crystals of calcium carbonate that catch the light and send it dancing throughout the interior of the pearl. The complexity of beautiful, prismatic crystals radiating from the center forms layers of concentric arcs, rings, or branching prisms.

Looking into a pearl with superior orient is like looking into a crystal ball. The eye looks through the surface and observes the aurora borealis of light within. The best way to observe the interaction of light is to hold a pearl in front of a neutral background, such as a white cloth. As light shines on the pearl, the idea is to look past the lustrous surface and into the layers themselves. The play of light from the glow within enchants the eye. Some people are even able to perceive the inner nucleus through the opalescent layers. Subtle yet profound, the quality of orient in a pearl increases its beauty and desirability a thousandfold.

In human terms, the orient is our most spiritual part. As we look inside, past the surface and into the depths of ourselves, we catch a glimpse of our own light, refracting and creating our brilliant orient—the glow of health, the blush of desire, the radiance of enthusiasm, and the passion for life. Some people are so filled with life that they shine from within. They have charisma, a strong invisible magnetism that irresistibly draws others to them.

The orient of the pearl represents our personal spiritual journey, and it supports the discovery of what is truly meaningful to you, to me, to all of us. Because of our uniqueness, there are as many different paths to spirit as there are human beings in the world. Each must find her own path, and each must act as a guide to others. We are little flames. We are lights along the way, beckoning each other, giving encouragement, smiling with shared understanding. However, we can only offer direction, not dictate it; the soul's quest is a journey so intimate, so personal, that no one can force it upon another. One must choose one's path, find the way, and proceed with courage and faith. Let the concept of the pearl's orient inspire you to magnify your own inner light until it shines like a beacon, illuminating your journey through life.

GRANDMOTHER TIME

I soften my eyes, slow my breathing, and allow my gaze to fall on the pearl I hold cupped in my hands. I breathe in and out deeply and just enjoy sitting quietly and feeling the weight and the smoothness of this beautiful pearl. I peer into it, letting my eyes go past the surface of the pearl and into the swirl of iridescent color beyond.

Nothing happens for quite a long time. I start to feel impatient—I shake my head a little, refocus, and concentrate again.

As I gaze into the pearl, the rounded edges disappear and I am drawn within. I look deeper and begin to see movement. As I follow the movement, a scene opens up to me and I am inside.

I see rolling waves, turquoise water, and a single wave breaking on the shore. I become aware that I don't actually have to look into the pearl anymore. Now the scene seems to unfold in front of me, around me.

Is the movement I see in the water the tail of a whale? I move toward the water and a mermaid swims past me.

Memories flash before me of swimming in a swimming pool and pretending to be a mermaid. All the freedom and delight of being a carefree child, floating gracefully and diving deep under the water, come flooding back to me.

"Good," she says, popping up near me. "You *do* remember me!"

"How could I forget?"

I walk into the water, enchanted. The mermaid takes my hand and together we dive under the water, swimming hard, pulsing our strong tails, moving at top speed. I feel myself laughing underwater. The sensation is exhilarating.

We swim on together, and I notice that the water gradually becomes a lighter blue as it gets shallower. The mermaid slows down a little. A huge cave awaits, and she takes me inside. It's very dark, but as my eyes adjust to the light I observe art, antiques, and fine tapestries on the walls.

Sitting in a rocking chair at the far end of the cave sits a small old merwoman. Her tail is a fine web of wrinkles and lines as intricate as old lace. She has been dozing in her chair, but now she wakes up.

"Hello, my daughters," she smiles. "Come closer so I can see you."

I swim over, and she reaches out her hand to greet me. I take her hand and can feel every tiny bone as she squeezes gently.

"Welcome, dear," she murmurs.

She wears strands and strands of pearls around her neck, twined in her long silver hair. The pearls of a long life filled with many wonderful memories encircle her neck, head, waist, arms, and stretch out across the floor. The pearls glow with inner beauty and light.

"Look inside," she urges. I look at the pearls and see a flicker inside each one. On closer inspection, I realize that a little scene is taking place inside each of the hundreds and thousands of pearls in the cave.

"Each pearl is a memory," Grandmother chuckles.

She lifts up one of her heavy pearl strands.

"Here, look," she says.

I take the strand, amazed at the size and substance of each pearl.

"They are heavy," I remark.

"What did you expect?" she laughs. "Each holds much life. Here, look at this one."

She chooses a pearl, and I look into it as if it were a crystal ball.

I see a scene of a young woman walking to work. She looks tired. She carries a heavy briefcase filled with work that she took home the night before.

"That looks like me," I sigh.

"That is you," she answers. She hands me another strand of pearls, and I see that each one contains a scene from my life. Some pearls show me as a little girl, others as a teenager, a wife. Finally, she hands me one last pearl, and I see that it's cloudy inside.

"I can't see this one, Grandmother. I want to see what is inside."

"Of course you can't see it. It's your future, and you haven't lived it yet . . ." The ancient merwoman hugs me, and I close my eyes and sigh.

"What does it all mean, Grandmother?" I collapse into her soft arms.

"It means that now it's your turn to share what you know."

With that, she is gone.

The scene becomes misty, and I pull myself out of my reverie to find that I am seated in my chair, holding a pearl cupped in my hands, looking deeply into it. I remember her words: *Share what you know.*

Meditation

Many of us long for connection to the divine; we ache for meaning in our lives, for a deeper sense of unity and purpose. The depth of our spiritual longing may send us into the world searching for answers, but ultimately the soul calls us home and invites us to look within. When we open our hearts we let light into our being. Spiritual light seeks a way inside, a way past our protective shells. Once we relax into the warmth of its nourishing glow, we begin to emanate a light of our own. The light ricochets off our thousands of layers, seeking the crystals of awareness, the fires of life force within us. That will to live, to grow, to understand, to give back what we have learned is what creates the orient of our lives.

When we open to the light of spirit, our inner being dances in the pearly sky. We delight in the beauty of the light as it passes into us, through us, and into all parts of our lives. To accept this healing, empowering light opens us to a larger light, the light of the sun, of the creation, of a power higher than ourselves. Life force compels us to let down our guard, to remove our shells, to let the light of love inside through the opening that the nucleus of change has created for us.

When we alter our perception this way, we are then able to see the many bumps in life as opportunities for growth—blessings from a higher power. In turn, you can bless these obstacles rather than struggling against them. By blessing a challenging situation or person, you diffuse potentially negative power and jump-start your own inner growth. When you bless something, you become free to learn from it.

Think about something in your life that may be causing you grief right now. Can you send a blessing to it? Can you give thanks for the opportunity to grow through this challenge? Try sending a blessing to a person who has disturbed you. If you can do this, you will be on your way to healing—and to creating a pearl.

Painful and hard lessons can bring us closer to our true nature; they can show us that we are not separate, that we are one, in effect, bringing us closer to God. The pearl is a shining light of spiritual perfection on the journey to finding truth. We turn to the higher power when all else fails, and we discover that our soul has been patiently waiting for us to discover it.

PEARLS OF WISDOM: All power comes from within.
The seed of our soul, the source of our connection with ourselves, with others, and with spirit is found within. Divine source is within.

Strength will come when we recognize that no one has authority over our own destiny and life's journey. We are responsible for making the highest and best choices for ourselves. We have the ultimate power to change—and we don't give our power to others. We claim our power. We reach inside, past all the layers of our mundane, day-to-day lives, and connect with that essential light, that shining pearl, which glows within.

FURTHER REFLECTION

Nucleus

❧ Do you feel you have travelled on a spiritual quest?

❧ When did it begin, and what were you in search of?

❧ What obstacles have hindered or contributed to your spiritual growth?

Layering

❧ Have there been mentors or teachers along the way who have helped you overcome obstacles on your path, spiritual or otherwise?

❧ Have you ever thanked your spiritual guides, either directly or by sharing what you've learned with others?

Awareness and Beauty

❧ What was your earliest thought of something existing beyond the physical world?

❧ What insights have you gained that sustain you each day?

Traditions of the Pearl

Throughout history, the pearl has been used as a metaphor for feminine virtue and fidelity. To the Greeks, the word pearl signified purity and loyalty to the marital bed. The Greek god Hymen, the god of marriage, is often depicted holding a strand of pearls, representing the marital bond between Eros (heart) and Psyche (mind).

The pearl is the jewel of choice for brides all over the world. It symbolizes innocence, purity, and loyalty—all characteristics that brides traditionally wish to convey to their husbands. Many brides wear a simple strand of white pearls or white pearl earrings, or both, and pearls are often used as adornment on wedding gowns. Pearls symbolize a happy marriage, and they are the anniversary gemstone for the third and thirtieth years of marriage.

In the South, there is a lovely tradition of giving a little girl a pearl each year on her birthday and on any other special occasion. The tradition continues until she has collected enough for a necklace to wear at her "sweet sixteen" birthday celebration. Eventually, she may wear it on her wedding day.

Pearl and moonstone are the official birthstones for people born in the month of June.

7

Perfection, Imperfection, and Sensuality

> And Krishna brought forth pearls
> from the depths of the sea
> to give his daughter on her wedding day.
> — *The Rig-Veda, c. 1000 B.C.*

Perfection and Imperfection

*S*ensual and satiny smooth, the pearl is heavenly to touch. But just as diamonds have flaws, pearls also have natural marks. It is an endearing aspect of their character.

Surface perfection refers to the skin of the pearl, which will usually have blemishes, blisters, dark spots, or other marks. These imperfections are referred to as "birthmarks." They are identifying characteristics that verify the pearl is not an imitation. Even top-grade pearls will show a few birthmarks.

Simulated pearls such as Majorica, faux, or "impostor" pearls and beads will have a perfectly smooth surface and are easily distinguished, even by the novice. You can test your own pearls by gently running a pearl along the top edge of your two front bottom teeth. Your teeth will feel a subtle sandpaper texture. Try running your teeth along a glass bead or fake pearl and then try the real pearl again. The fake pearl or glass bead will feel perfectly smooth. The edge of the tooth easily detects the infinitesimally small edges of the layers and feels the roughness on the surface of the real pearl. Something essential is missing from those things created artificially, and we sense it from somewhere deep within ourselves. It's no surprise, then, that we are naturally suspicious of individuals who seem too perfect, too smooth, too polished on the surface. Human beings are not perfect. We, too, are made special by our birthmarks, beauty marks, freckles, and other identifying characteristics. The pearl gently nudges us to accept our flaws, to perceive them as marks of our personality. Treasure your identity—you are one in a million.

To evaluate surface perfection, pearls are examined against both white and dark backgrounds, and in different types of light. But just as with our own individual character-istics, all the other criteria—shape, size, color, luster, orient—are as important as perfection. As we know, sacrificing one criterion, such as luster, in order to have a more "flawless" surface, will diminish the overall value of a gem. And isn't it interesting that high luster can actually conceal imperfections to a large degree, just as a sparkling personality can render an individual's physical shortcomings invisible?

When we look into the deepest part of ourselves, we must also remember that while we all have flaws, we are also ultimately expressions of spiritual perfection. We are the drops of water that combine to make the ocean. Each of us, in our uniqueness, represents a facet of divine energy. As loving creations of the giver of life, we walk in grace and beauty, as does every living creature.

Meditation

Imagine that you are sitting in front of a huge tray of pearls—thousands and thousands of beautiful pearls, glimmering in the light. Each is a different shape and size; each has bumps, swirls, and circles; each has dimples and bulges, roughness and smoothness; each glows with a beauty that is rare and unique.

As you gaze at the tray, your eye is drawn to just one. It is special and unique, and somehow you feel it is *your* pearl. It pulls you closer and closer. You gaze at it in wonder. It is not perfect; it has its own expression of beauty.

You pick it up and feel its satiny smoothness against your fingers. As you cradle it gently in your hand, you see how deserving it is of your appreciation. Examining all sides of it, you smile as you encounter its birthmarks and imperfections, marks that make it all the more rare and precious.

As you admire this lovely example of nature's mastery, imagine that you are this pearl. You have spent years becoming this rare gift of nature. Allow yourself to associate your flaws and imperfections with those of the pearl, gently becoming aware that your beauty marks, your unique qualities, and even your imperfections are what also make *you* special and rare. Accept this pearl as your teacher of the self-acceptance and love that you deserve. To accept yourself, to honor your own inner beauty, and to love yourself are the building blocks of contentment. Celebrate yourself, just as you are.

Sensuality

The pearl is closely associated with fertility. Oyster shell is referred to as *mother* of pearl, and the creation of a pearl is called a birth. To the Romans, the pearl was synonymous with love and pleasure. The ancient Greeks associated the pearl with Aphrodite, the goddess of love. Aphrodite, or Venus, as the Romans called her, is said to have risen from the ocean on the foam of the sea. Legend tells that as she stepped out of the sea at her birth, she shook off droplets of water, which then hardened and fell back into the sea as pearls. Thus, pearls were thought to promote erotic love, passion, and marital bliss.

We have much in common with the pearl: the complexity of its sensuality, its irresistibly smooth skin, juxtaposed with its status as a symbol of virginity and purity. We are often expected to be both virtuous and sexually passionate. Women's roles in history fluctuate between these two extremes, and this mixed message is a burden shared by the pearl—perhaps another reason we respond to its allure. It reminds us of the paradox we are supposed to embody: virgin, temptress, mother, symbol of both fertility and reproduction as well as saintliness. Is the pearl a symbol of chastity and faith? Or is it the epitome of lust, carnal and passionate, emerging from the wet lips of the mother oyster, a gleaming gem of transcendent sexual pleasure? The pearl is both, just as women are both. The most accepted roles both for women and for pearls are extreme. How is it conceivable that a pearl can be both innocent and exquisitely sexual? How can a woman be both saint and prostitute?

The surface smoothness of the pearl is like the smoothness of a lover's skin. Pearls make us feel good about ourselves. They enhance the skin, the face, and the eyes. They sit comfortably against the skin, caressing the neck, fingers, and ears. They seduce. The silky texture easily brings thoughts of passionate love to mind, especially if the pearl has been a gift from one's ardent lover. The pearl holds the promise of hidden treasures beneath the sea—and beneath the sheets.

WORSHIPPING THE MOON GODDESS

I look deeply into the pearl in my palm. I begin to see movement. As I follow it, the scene opens up to me and I am inside.

I see the full moon in the night sky; a madwoman wanders in the night, the sorceress ever wakeful. The moon is menses, female, fertile, lunar pulsing waning and waxing, shrinking and expanding, ever growing, changing the tides, the ebb and flow of all Earth's waters: ocean, blood, semen, tears, streams, and sweat.

The moon, infinite and feminine, charges the Earth night after night, driving poets to brilliance, sages to speak in tongues, oracles to flame, and men to hide indoors. The night, in which crimes are committed, in which life is conceived in the throes of passion—all over the world, all at once, every night.

In all the houses and temples and caves and hovels and convertibles and tents of the world, men and woman make love in the moonlight, and life flows into the Earth's aching void. Love and life regenerated in the night, in the glimmering magical silver-mooned spellbound soul time.

The shining moon is a healer, gliding gracefully, eternally through space. Dancing with vulnerability and silver sensitivity, she becomes the priestess and guardian of the moon temple, worshipper of the moon goddess, of the moon itself.

Moon, reflecting sun's light, guiding through the darkness, illuminating the madness, celebrating the harvest.

The scene becomes misty, and I come out of my trance, seated in my chair, still holding the pearl in my palm.

PEARL
Sacred art
From love's lost pain,
Symbol of transformation,
The pearl.

Remaking irritation,
Past hurt is gone,
Only the spirit,
Beauty, softness
And light remain.

For years she layers it
Cell by cell, micromillimeter,
She spins the sculptor's lathe
That is her body, her flesh.

Layers of gossamer moonbeams,
Silvery spider webs,
Light refracting
Cover the tiny nucleus,
Remake and create
Rapture!

**PEARLS OF WISDOM: Now is the time for acceptance
and appreciation.**

Decide right now to change your need for, or your perception of, perfection. On the surface, nothing is perfect—a testimony to our individuality; and yet, spiritually, everything is perfect. We live in a world of no mistakes.

Celebrate your body, your life, and your beauty marks. Cease judging and criticizing. Shine your light so bright that you dazzle the world. Focus on the larger picture, the bigger dream, the overwhelming beauty of life rather than on the tiny details. Place your attention on your contributions rather than on your deficiencies.

Accentuate the positive, like the gem connoisseur who sees a pearl's birthmarks as a testament to its natural beauty. Accept yourself and love yourself, for you are a perfect creation of nature, and your distinguishing marks add to your value and rarity.

FURTHER REFLECTION

Nucleus

🐚 Do you judge yourself by strict standards and high expectations?

Layering

🐚 Choose a facet of yourself that you feel is a flaw. Can you forgive yourself for it? Can you embrace it, remembering that you express the spiritual perfection of creation just as you are?

🐚 Are you connected with your sensuality? What can you do, either alone or with a partner, that will make you feel sexy and sensuous?

Awareness and Beauty

🐚 Can you see the beauty in imperfection? How are you beautifully imperfect?

🐚 What would your perfect life look like? If you were to realistically adjust your idea of perfection, might you find that your real life is closer to perfect than you think?

THE POWER OF THE PEARL

One legend has it that Cleopatra, queen of Egypt, crushed a large pearl given to her by her lover Mark Antony, and together they drank it in a glass of wine as a testimonial to their undying love.

In another version of this famous legend, she removed one of her pearl earrings, dissolved it in a glass of wine, and drank it to win a wager with Mark Antony. She had bet him that she could consume the wealth of an entire country in just one meal. By dissolving a pearl in her glass of wine, she did indeed drink the wealth of a nation and thus win the wager.

It is also said that Cleopatra offered the matching earring to Mark Antony if he would do the same. Astonished, he declined his dinner—and the matching pearl. The two pearls were apparently worth an estimated 60 million sesterces, or approximately $9,375,000. Cleopatra thereby demonstrated her extreme wealth and, most of all, her power as a woman and a queen.

8

Value and Rarity

> The richest merchandise of all, the most sovereign
> commodity throughout the whole world,
> are these pearls.
> — *Pliny the Elder (23–79 A.D.)*, Historia Naturalis

*I*magine living in ancient times, walking along the seashore, and finding a half-open oyster on the sand in front of you. Opening the crusty shell, you discover a large gleaming pearl shimmering in the sunlight. Such a gift of the gods would stagger your mind and delight your senses. This pearl would have the power to transform your life, instantly making you one of the richest and most honored members of your village.

In the first century A.D., Roman general Aulus Vitellius is said to have financed an entire military campaign on the proceeds from selling just one of his mother's pearl earrings.

In the royal courts, the pearl was a coveted sign of power, wealth, and distinction. One need only to wander through the art museums and castles of Europe to see paintings in which pearls in great abundance adorn the ears, necks, heads, and costumes of monarchs and nobility. Pearls have been loved and cherished by many queens of Europe. Portraits of Queen Elizabeth I of England, the Virgin Queen, always portray her bedecked in the pearls she avidly collected.

Even with the pearl farms, there are not enough pearls created in the vast oceans of the world to meet the demand for them. It is this demand that gives pearls their incredible value, and it is their rarity that makes them precious—but how do we determine the value?

In the world of fine jewelry, the system of grading used by gemologists to evaluate and price each pearl is based on the six criteria, but these strict criteria are only for determining monetary value. There is no way to evaluate the symbolic, emotional, and personal worth of the pearl. Those are simply priceless.

Having used the six grading criteria as doors to new understanding about ourselves, we now take time to consider what all these factors mean in terms of our worth. Value, money, and wealth—these are often intertwined and difficult areas in women's lives. Our attitudes about money are sometimes related to what we feel we deserve. In many households, women manage family bills and the check-book, and yet they discount their strengths in this area. Ever practical, women are more often savers than investors. Perhaps because of their traditional roles of dependency on others, they fear there will not be enough money or resources to get by.

In my many years of working in the Black Pearl Galleries, I have seen men spend very large sums of money on their wives and girlfriends. And I have seen men spend large amounts on jewelry for themselves. But rarely have I seen a woman buy extravagantly for herself. I have wondered if a woman can give herself the same kind of total acknowledgment as she might receive from a man. Obviously she wouldn't need to have a man present to validate her if she was completely confident in her own decisions, in her own taste. Yet it happens so rarely. Are women simply more frugal? Or is there something deeper? It has made me wonder about value, and rarity, and worthiness of a reward. How does this relate to a woman's power, to her self-acceptance, and to her self-love?

At a time in my life when I had an uneasy relationship with money, I used to have a recurring nightmare every time I would use an ATM machine. I imagined it would say

"Declined! You have no more money at all." Irrational visions of myself as a bag lady on the streets of Los Angeles would flood my mind. I have been fortunate enough to replace my bag-lady fear with the reality of becoming co-owner of a lovely pearl business. It wasn't an easy transition. I had to give up a lot of mindless things I used to squander my time on. I had to learn to focus, to move beyond my wall of fear. I set about learning all I could, and in the past ten years I have been able to blast through my money fears, learning about real estate, mortgages, investments, banking, corporations, and business in ways I never dreamed possible. Once I accepted that money is a gift, once I allowed money to flow into my life, I saw it bring pleasure to others and myself in ways I'd never imagined.

I no longer believe that money has power over my happiness, but I do believe that it represents freedom, choices, and generosity. I have learned to see myself as a "fountain of prosperity" with the money I make flowing up through me and then sprinkling and splashing on all those close to me.

Greed and Waste

In ancient times, pearls were found in the Persian Gulf and the Red Sea as well as along the coasts of India and Ceylon, the Middle East, South and Central America, Burma, and Vietnam. All of those natural pearl-oyster beds are now extinct, fished out long ago by overzealous pearl merchants.

In the fourth century B.C., pearls were found in Egypt and Greece. But the Western world had its real introduction to pearls when Alexander the Great conquered all the lands to the east and west. He defeated Darius III, the last king of Persia, and gathered a fabulous booty that included some extraordinarily valuable pearls. The Persian Gulf was home to some of the world's richest pearl fisheries, and the Persian rulers had huge fortunes in pearls. The waters of the Red Sea and the Indian Ocean were thriving with pearl oysters. The European expansion to the New World brought the discovery of pearls in Central American waters by Christopher Columbus and Vasco de Balboa, and pearls became the New World's most valuable export. In Europe, the Americas were known as "The Land of Pearls," and in Panama and Venezuela pearls were in abundant supply—at least until Columbus and Balboa arrived. By the seventeenth century, the greed and lust for these pearls depleted the natural pearl-oyster populations. For each pearl harvested, thousands of oysters were sacrificed in the search. More recently, many species of pearl-producing oysters were endangered until they came under the protection of local governments who could see that a precious commodity was being threatened by overfishing.

Here the message of the pearl is to not be greedy. Don't take more than you need. Excessive greed can eventually wipe out the natural supply of most anything. In John Steinbeck's famous novel *The Pearl*, Kino the pearl diver finds the largest, most beautiful pearl ever seen. For him it symbolizes the potential for escape from a life of desperate poverty, but it brings sadness and pain to his life when everyone he knows and trusts manipulates to steal it from him. Some people interpret this story to mean that the pearl brings bad luck. The real meaning, however, is that it is not the pearl itself but the human reaction to it—the insatiable greed and the lust for wealth—that can bring extraordinary pain.

So be conscious of your assets and your talents. Be grateful and appreciate the gifts they truly are. And don't misspend or waste the gifts you have.

Meditation

So, what does it take for us to truly value ourselves? What do we do, achieve, learn, or create in order to give ourselves the credit we deserve? There is only one version of me here on this planet, and there is only one version of you. You are like that pearl of great price; you are rare and possess incalculable value. The lives of every one of us are priceless. Each of us deserves limitless health, limitless joy, and limitless wealth. You deserve the best life has to offer.

Here, the message of the pearl is that there are no boundaries, no limits to our value, and no limits to how much bounty we can create in our lives. Remove all limitation when determining your own value and that of others.

"Be like me," the pearl proclaims. "Be rare beyond all others. Be desirable and sought after and highly prized! Be admired and wealthy and filled with life's true riches." In the book of Matthew in the Bible, Jesus warns us, "Neither cast ye your pearls before swine, lest they trample them under their feet, and turn again and rend you." In other words, value yourself, and don't squander the pearls of your beauty, rarity, wisdom, and strength.

PEARLS OF WISDOM: **There are no limitations.**

Believe in your own value. Experience yourself as priceless and limitless. You are a fountain of prosperity, happiness, love, giving, and receiving. There is no end to your potential, to what you can contribute. Treasure the precious pearl that is your life.

Why do we so often think that what we have is not enough, not right, not the thing we really need? Why do we question and demean the gifts we are given in life and in love? Why the constant striving to be more, to have more? What if it's enough? What if *you* are enough—cherished, special, priceless, unlimited in value, beautiful, and unique? Just like the pearls!

FURTHER REFLECTION

Nucleus

- Have you ever undervalued yourself? What is it at those times which makes you feel that you are of less value than other people?
- Are you comfortable in your relationship with money? What would you like to see change, and what might be a first step toward that goal?

Layering

❧ In what ways have you tried to give yourself the same degree of value and support that you give to others?

Awareness and Beauty

❧ What gift can you give yourself in order to acknowledge your tremendous worth? What gift will announce to the world how much you value yourself?

The Magic of Pearls

Pearls are believed by many cultures to possess the magical powers of love, protection, prosperity, and luck as well as to be conducive to feelings of peacefulness, compassion, and healing. Some cultures believe that pearls also increase psychic ability.

Mystically, pearls symbolize the center of creation and the universe. They are connected to lunar energy and especially to the full moon. Since the moon and ocean tides are so closely connected, pearls are astrologically most closely linked to the moon, though they are also associated with the planetary influences of Venus and Mercury.

All oceanic deities, such as Neptune and Poseidon, are associated with the pearl. In the early Saxon religion, pearls were thought to be the congealed tears of Freya, the goddess of love and fertility.

Pearls are always associated with magical mermaids. Swimmers in the oceans have worn pearls as a magical protection against sharks. Pearls have also been thought to ward off demons, lengthen life, promote fertility, preserve health, and increase strength and physical power.

9

Glamour and Magic

The unicorn was white, with hoofs of
silver and graceful horn of pearl . . .
— *T. H. White*

$\mathscr{I}$n myth and legend, magic
and mystery, alchemy and religion, the pearl is a source of
wonder, revered and even worshipped. Evocative, beautiful, unexplainable, it has been one of mankind's obsessions
since ancient times. With its magical allure, the pearl—this
miracle of nature—haunts our dreams and fills our waking
hours with beauty.

Working in our pearl stores, I have watched over and
over as men and women become curious about pearls,
then bewitched by them, and finally drawn to the pearl of
their dreams. I have observed that their choice is rarely a
logical decision. Rather, it's as though that pearl were
silently calling to them, reaching out to claim its owner.
More than a choice, it is an emotional desire. When the

person is enticed by a pearl, it becomes almost an obsession—a heeding of the siren's call. I celebrate this discovery because I see it as an awakening to something intimate and personal. Pearls represent our sense of self, our individual style. They appeal emotionally and aesthetically. Whether it is the largest, rarest, and most expensive pearl or the gift of a tiny pearl to a young girl, they inspire and uplift. They make us feel glamorous, powerful, and special.

Glamour

The novelist Horace Walpole wrote of Queen Elizabeth I, "A pale Roman nose, a head of hair loaded with crowns and powdered with diamonds, a vast ruff, a vaster fardingale, and a bushel of pearls, are the features by which everyone knows at once the pictures of Queen Elizabeth."

The pearl is called the queen of gems, and many queens in addition to Elizabeth I have been absolutely obsessed with pearls—most famously Cleopatra of Egypt; Isabella of Spain; Mary Queen of Scots; Marie de Médici, queen of Henry IV of France; Marie Antoinette of France; Eugénie of Holland; Josephine, empress of France; Queen Victoria; Queen Elizabeth II, and the Queen Mother.

Stylish and glamorous women throughout the centuries have posed for portraits and been photographed wearing pearls. And each remarkable woman has added her personal style to the legendary pearl. Coco Chanel, Josephine Baker, Louise Brooks, Theda Bara, Jackie Onassis, Sharon Stone, Lady Diana, and Elizabeth Taylor—each has loved pearls and made them part of her own distinctive style. Each has brought her own fashion sense and drama to the pearls she wore and changed the way other women feel about pearls and about themselves. Norma Jean Baker knew how to turn adversity into art. She took the painful childhood that was the nucleus of her being, layered it with beauty and sexuality, and transformed herself into Marilyn Monroe, the most famous sex goddess of the 1950s. Often seen wearing a little black cocktail dress and a long strand of white pearls, she would seductively twirl this luxurious strand that hung to her navel.

Film star and legendary beauty Lauren Bacall also adorns herself with glorious pearls. She often wears large pearl necklaces in her photos, as do Candace Bergen and Maria Shriver.

It was Elizabeth Taylor who brought Tahitian black pearls into the jewelry lexicon for many women. As an avid collector of jewelry and gems, she developed a dynamic perfume dynasty by producing scents that she names after her beloved jewels. White Diamonds, her first, pioneered the way for the introduction of her Black Pearls perfume in 1996. When she appeared on television and in advertising campaigns wearing luscious strands of Tahitian black pearls, she caused a sensation. Women who'd never heard of a black pearl now wanted one. In one ad, emerging from the water, her hair slicked back, wearing exotic black pearl earrings and a strand of huge, round Tahitian pearls, Taylor looked like a goddess. Especially after her years of failed marriages, hardships, health challenges, and near-fatal bouts of addiction, she was Venus once again rising from the sea—renewed, youthful, and gorgeous.

For the millions of women who grew up watching this icon, the image was captivating, and the effect, dramatic. The perfume sold well, and it immediately launched an interest in black pearls. The gem went from being an exotic rarity to a jewelry wardrobe staple. Women everywhere were learning that they identified with pearls, whose wide range of colors, shapes, and sizes can make anyone feel like a star.

Magic

Treasured by royalty, stolen by pirates, and hoarded in secret dragons' lairs, legendary mystical, restorative, and healing powers have been attributed to the pearl. Emerging from the depths of the sea, mermaids evoke the ocean's mystery and aquatic sensuality. The mermaid loves pearls. She drapes herself in pearl necklaces, threads pearls through her hair, and holds a pearl-studded mirror.

My earliest pangs of spiritual hunger came from listening to fairy tales. The dragon of Western fairy tales usually lives in a cave where he sleeps on his mounds of stolen treasure. Surrounded by chests of gold and strands of pearls, he sleeps peacefully until bothered by a courageous knight out to prove his valor. Inspired by these stories, I spent hours searching for fairies and treasure in our backyard, looking under bushes, in the dewy morning grass, in the spaces between flowers and rocks. I loved to sit beneath the flowering bottlebrush, let my eyes soften, and gaze under the leaves until I could see the fairy rings where magical courts convened.

Our backyard was a place of wonder, built by my father over many levels of brick pathways and flower beds. There were two apple trees halfway down the brick path to "the lower forty." A side yard seemed a no man's land of potential darkness, stickers, and unknown evil. Grape vines and lavender wisteria hung from overhead trellises above the brick patios that were connected by brick stairways, bridges, and paths. Sitting quietly in one of the flower beds, gazing out from under blonde bangs, was a young girl of four or five, searching for magic. I knew it was there; I could feel it.

Where is the part of you that looks at the world with wonder? Can you remember being awestruck by the mystery and beauty of fireflies dancing in the air and twinkle-lights encircling lacy tree limbs? Pearls are a tangible way to connect with the child within. Their magic reminds us that our logical minds do not have all the answers. There is a hidden world more strange and bizarre. Like the twilight moments between waking and dreaming, this magical realm calls to us.

The world of reality and the world of fantasy have shadowy boundaries populated by spirits, memories, flights of fancy. In the magical land we suspend disbelief. We are no longer skeptics. We courageously embrace our amazement and celebrate the unknown. We surrender to the hope that wishes do come true, we clap our hands to prove our belief in fairies, and we swim like a mermaid in the waters of our soul.

The pearl is a magical gem born of these mystical landscapes. Its beauty defies logic, its birth a true mystery. No matter how man longs to control its characteristics, it is not within human power. The pearl dazzles us with its mystique. It beckons us to remember what it is like to believe in magic.

I love the ancient Chinese legend claiming that oysters become pregnant by thunder. The Asian rain god, the Sky Dragon, releases droplets from its mouth during thunderstorms, and some of the droplets settle in oyster shells that lay open during those storms. After raindrops fall into the oysters' mouths, pearls grow, nourished by moonlight. The Chinese traditionally believe that pearls fall to earth when dragons fight in the clouds above during storms. Chinese carvings, screens, and paintings often depict the majestic dragon holding a prized pearl in its mouth or claws, a symbol of immortality and heaven, magic, and luck.

In ancient mythology, the pearl is closely associated with the moon, a symbol of purity and solitude, the mover of ocean tides. It was believed that this gem from the sea had the power to communicate with the moon and that the soul of the pearl and the soul of the moon were one.

The mystical associations of the pearl include goddesses from many different cultures. In Hinduism, there is a story of Indira's Net, a huge invisible net stretching over the earth, dotted by billions of pearls that gleam at the crossing points, each pearl representing a soul. Diana, the Roman goddess of light, the moon, and the wild, is closely identified with the Greek goddess Artemis. She loves to roam the mountains with a companion group of nymphs. Because pearls are often associated with the moon, Diana and Artemis are also goddesses of pearls. Hina, the Hawaiian goddess of beauty, the sea, and the moon, is associated with water and pearls. She brings light to the darkness and represents the positive in all things. Worshippers of Hina call upon her to bring light and beauty into their lives, honoring her by accepting the happy and beautiful sides of life.

MOON AND FOUR STARS
It was a full moon bursting
With silvery songs,
Magic music floating on whispery clouds
Shaping . . . unshaping.

Sudden brilliance of night's first stars
All in a line,
Miraculous pageant!
Sparkling pearls, four in a straight row.

Tinkling, joyous quartet of sopranos
Stole the moon's attention all night long.
Shadows walked the silver sands.

Shimmery, pearly moon
and four stars.

PEARLS OF WISDOM: **Now is the moment of magic.**
There is magic in each moment. Take action right now to change what is not working in your life. Believe in the miracle of transformation. Take a leap of faith! Dare to dream big, be different, try something new, create something magical from nothing.

Make a wish, sing a song, become a legend. Change is growth, and growth is life. Come alive, make a new choice, follow your passion. Dive into your soul and bring forth pearls and magic!

FURTHER REFLECTION

Nucleus

🐚 Do you recall a sense of magic from your childhood? Did you believe in magical creatures, fairies, unicorns, mermaids, or monsters?

🐚 If you no longer believe in magic, what made you stop believing?

Layering

🐚 As an adult, what do you do to tap into a sense of wonder and magic?

🐚 When was the last time you let yourself feel fabulously glamorous?

Awareness and Beauty

🐚 Can you find a way to let your imagination run wild? To indulge your secret, glamorous alter-ego?

🐚 Why not throw a costume party? Go wild on Hallowe'en or Mardi Gras? Do you have a friend with whom you could dress up for a day and pretend to be someone different, just for fun?

HYMN OF PROTECTION

Born of the wind, the atmosphere, the lightning, and the light, may this pearl shell, born of gold, protect us from straits!...With the shell [we conquer] disease and poverty, with the shell, too, the Sadanvas. The shell is our universal remedy; the pearl shall protect us from straits!...The bone of the gods turned into pearl; that, animated, dwells in the waters. That do I fasten upon thee unto life, luster, strength, longevity, unto a life lasting a hundred autumns. May the amulet of pearl protect thee!

— India's *Atharva-Veda*, c. 500 B.C.

10

The Ocean's Legacy

Neptune's beauty, ocean gem,
Receive nature's gift and ascend.

*W*ater represents fluidity, uniting with the elements and with the divine. It is a necessary element of life, the primordial birthplace of earthly creation. We are launched into the world from watery wombs, baptized in water; every organ in our body needs water to thrive.

Water is elemental but tangible, unlike air. Its currents cleanse us. Immersed in water, we find renewal, rebirth, refreshment, and a new beginning as we let the past wash away. Fluidity is power; we learn to be flexible rather than rigid. As we face life's challenges, we learn to respond rather than react, to flow with them rather than resist.

Imagine yourself as a river making its way to the sea. Nothing stops water from flowing to where it wants to go.

Even the largest mountain is slowly dissolved by water as erosion makes its slow and powerful changes. Let the image of water sustain you. Allow it to refresh and inspire and renew. Water is life itself. Formidable tsunami, jet streams, forty-foot waves, falling rain—water's power and strength is awe-inspiring. The more we can imitate the flow and flexibility of water, the easier our lives will become.

Pearls are born in water—in the oceans, lakes, rivers, and streams—and all pearl oysters need water to survive. Once the oyster has received the nucleus, it is placed in the warm, shallow lagoon to heal. Bathed in the healing water, it begins to recover. The oyster mends, repairs damage, and copes with crisis.

Perhaps it is due to this association with the healing powers of the ocean that every culture of the world has considered the pearl to be medicinal. The most commonly held belief was that the pearl conferred great vitality upon its owner. During the Middle Ages, gallant knights often wore pearls onto the battlefield, believing these magical gems would protect them. In China and many other Asian countries, pearls are crushed and sold in powders and pills as well as in creams and ointments. The Chinese treat toxicity and diseases of the eye and ear with pearls. In Persia, pearls are used to cure indigestion, hemorrhaging, and malaria. It is told that in feudal Japan, physicians treated their noble clients with pearl ointments and tablets. Pearls were prescribed for longevity and as a love potion. In India, the pearl is used to break fever. The many references to the pearl protecting us made in the "Hymn of Protection" recorded in India's *Atharva-Veda* are indicative of the long-held beliefs that pearls convey wide-ranging powers of protection.

Turning the nucleus, rolling it and moving it around inside its body, the mother of the pearl begins to create. Adding layer upon layer of nacre—constantly, without rest—the pearl oyster accepts and adapts to its challenge and creates its protection from the invasion. The oyster protects its sensitive inner flesh by layering *itself* around the irritant, transforming the irritant into a part of itself and into something new. But it takes years for the nucleus to become a pearl. The process cannot be rushed. It is a daily challenge.

How do we human beings go about achieving transformation in our lives? We, too, roll a new concept around in our being, seeking ways to accept and embrace it. We mull it over, get accustomed to the intrusion, and ultimately transform it. We dig deep into our inner selves, pray for guidance, and muster strength to make changes. We adapt.

We create. We flow with the changes. Each trial, each hardship, serves as a nucleus for the pearls that comprise our gems of experience, knowledge, and awareness.

A Lasting Legacy

Pearls are an heirloom to pass along to daughters and granddaughters. They continue to share their beauty far into the future.

If well taken care of, pearls are extremely durable. They thrive on the moisture and oil they pick up from lying against our skin, and the luster and beauty of the pearl becomes noticeably improved with wear—a gentle reminder to all of us that if we take good care and treat ourselves well, we too can improve with age. Locked in a safe-deposit box, pearls can crack and become dehydrated and yellowed over time. Pearls need to be worn, loved, and enjoyed. Like us, they need to get out in the open.

Revering life, respecting this gift we have all been given, is the most important discovery of our later years. We become increasingly aware of the beauty and spirit of life, and we realize that nothing matters except love. The love we have given and the love we have shared is all there is. These are the thoughts that can fill our hearts with joy.

Our own lives, lived vibrantly and fully, are an inspiration to those who come after. The seeds of our creativity are planted in future generations. The works of love and beauty we create still resonate when we are gone. The meaning of our lives will be revealed by the things we did to make the world around us a little better. Did we make a difference? Did we contribute in a positive way to humankind and Mother Earth?

Time is relentless, sending seasons that change. The new is born as the old dies. That is the way of nature. But we can leave behind the gifts of our knowledge, the gifts of our accomplishments, the dreams of others that we helped to come true. The next generation stands on our shoulders. Memories, lustrous and rare, are the gems of our life's journey, and our soul is the thread that strings them together. In the eternal present there is always time to create memories for your family to treasure. There is always time to ponder the questions, to find out what it is we want to give, and to leave a mark.

Nothing better illustrates the importance of seizing the day than this wonderful story:

A seventy-two-year-old woman decided she wanted to get her degree in law. She signed up to attend the local college and was enjoying her classes.

One day she saw an old friend on the street and told her that she had returned to school. The friend was shocked. "My God," said the friend, "you will be eighty years old when you graduate!"

The woman smiled and answered, "I'll be eighty whether I graduate or not."

Time passes, and the tides continue to come in and go out. With the advancing years, we grow calmer, softer, deeper, and wiser. Like the waves, we are part of the ocean's caress. On the beaches of life, we become one with every creature, every pearl, every grain of sand. We delve into the treasure chests of our deepest soul and let the sea carry us home.

Seen through the tides of time, the gathered seashells of experience, the challenges of our past begin to make sense. "Ah, yes," we muse, "I had to go through that in order to discover these other gifts." The difficulties of our lives, each a nucleus, grow into a lovely strand of the pearls of our new wisdom and strengths.

The pearl teaches us to transform adversity into beauty, to heal ourselves in the process, and to use this knowledge to strengthen and protect ourselves. The pearl is a symbol for healing ourselves, our loved ones, and our world. It is a spiritual teacher and a metaphor for the human experience.

THE KISS OF TIME

Did it matter
that I walked this beach?
Danced this earth?
Ran this way?
Did it make a difference?
At all?

Did I leave a legacy?
A temple?
A family?
Have I left my mark?
Should I leave a mark?

The pearl's layered beauty
Leaves a treasure behind.
My life was my treasure
The kiss of time.

PEARLS OF WISDOM: Abundance may be invited in.
You are an entity as vast as the ocean, as limitless as the universe; there is no end to what you may create for yourself. Once you know your strength, you may not only accept and

embrace change but feel free to seek it out. With focus and clarity, search for new knowledge, master new skills, see new things. With each experience you open yourself to another world of possibility. Give to yourself and others with joy and freedom, and invite the universe to do the same.

FURTHER REFLECTION

Nucleus

 Is there anything you have left undone that you could begin today?

 Do you think about the legacy you will leave behind?

Layering

 What are you doing now to enrich that legacy?

Awareness and Beauty

 What are the most meaningful memories you have been given by those you have loved?

Mahalo

*T*hank you for joining me on the Path of the Pearl. It is my sincere wish that you have gained inspiration from these pages and that the symbol of the pearl will assist you in dealing with the challenges of your life. I offer this book to you as a testimonial to the fighting spirit and transformational abilities that we human beings share with the queen of gems, the pearl.

Mahalo—Thank You

Appendix:
Pearls, Lasting Treasures

Pearl Passion

*W*hen each culture reaches its pinnacle of art, power, and sophistication, the pearl is cherished and sought after. Pearl necklaces have been found dating back to 3000 B.C. And while there is ample research to prove that pearls have enjoyed constant popularity since then, there have also been several distinct pearl crazes in history.

The first was during the Roman Empire, at the time of Julius Caesar. The Romans were at the peak of their expansion, wealth, and power, and the entire culture was mad for pearls. In ancient Rome, pearls were considered the ultimate symbol of wealth and social standing. The value was so high that just one exceptionally exquisite pearl could fund an entire war effort.

The second pearl craze was in Europe during the Renaissance. As a result of the great explorations of the New

113

World, the Spanish royalty became wealthy from the pearls found in the Americas by explorers such as Columbus and Balboa. During the Renaissance, the insatiable lust for pearls was also amply displayed by the painters of the time. Queen Elizabeth I, painted many times during her reign of England, was always shown wearing ropes of pearls from her immense pearl collection.

The third pearl craze swept Paris and the United States in the 1920s. Popularized by such well-known figures as film star Theda Bara and cabaret performer Josephine Baker, pearls caught fire and became the most treasured fashion accessory in every woman's jewelry box.

The fourth pearl craze is upon us right now. Pearls of all varieties have risen in popularity in the past ten years. They are top sellers in jewelry stores in the United States, and women all over the world are buying and wearing them in record numbers. One need only open a fashion magazine to see models and celebrities rich and famous wearing pearls of all varieties.

Pearls are simply a fashion basic. They represent a time-less fashion aesthetic of exquisite style. They are treasured for generations and are passed down from mothers and grand-mothers. A strand of white cultured pearls is a must for every woman's collection. It can go from the office to a wedding reception, from church to evening wear. Many of our mothers taught us this lesson, and as a result, many women of my generation at first rejected pearls as being too conservative or old-fashioned. Little did we know that the pearl's appeal would far outlast our fleeting tastes. Bridging the generation gap, huge luscious South Seas and Tahitian pearls—exotic, rare, unique, and more dramatic than their Japanese counter-parts—have captured the fancy of baby boomers.

Many women have inherited pearls, or have been given them as gifts from husbands or boyfriends, or have surren-dered and purchased at least one strand of pearls them-selves, and now they are interested in finding out how to wear and enjoy them in new, more modern ways.

Pearl Harvest

The harvesting of pearls takes place once or twice a year. It is a grueling, exhausting process of bringing every oyster up out of the water, relaxing them so they will naturally open their shells, and then gently removing the pearls—if there are any.

Over 50 percent of the oysters will have nothing to show for the years of work the farmer spent tending and cherishing them. Of the 50 percent that do produce, approximately 20 percent of those oysters will produce pearls suitable for the world jewelry market. But only 2 percent of the harvest will have the color, iridescence, and luster considered to be the finest quality by gem dealers and appraisers. When we travel to the pearl farms and to the pearl auctions, we buy only the pearls in that narrow 2 percent to make into jewelry for our customers. The sub-quality pearls are thrown back into the ocean or crushed and made into healing products or face powders.

Variety

Worldwide, over seventy-two types of pearl-producing oysters can be found, and there are many different varieties of pearls. The major types of pearls, both freshwater and saltwater, are born of mollusks, a family that includes oysters, mussels, and clams. Freshwater pearls come from mussels, the most abundant of which grow in the clear streams and rivers of China. Many freshwater pearls are produced in each mussel at the same time. The freshwater pearl industry is thriving and pearl production is booming.

Oysters produce saltwater pearls, one at a time, and they take much longer to grow. This makes the pearls more rare and more expensive. For those who cannot afford salt-water South Seas, Tahitian, or Akoya pearls, freshwater pearls are very affordable and available in every jewelry store. American freshwater pearls grow in great abundance in the Mississippi and Tennessee rivers and surrounding streams. Biwa freshwater pearl oysters grow in Lake Biwa, Japan, and are scarcest due to the pollution of the lake.

South Seas pearls from eastern Australia are huge, lustrous, expensive, and in high demand. Tahitian black-lipped oysters, from the tiny islands and coral atolls of French Polynesia, produce pearls in a rainbow of natural colors. They are extremely large, exquisite, exotic, and rare.

Akoya pearl oysters grow in the ocean surrounding Japan. These pearls are the most well-known variety. They are small- to medium-size, round, white pearls and are most often used in strands.

Tahitian black pearls, the rarest gems on earth, are considered by many to be the world's most beautiful pearls. One hundred times more rare than white ones, these black pearls are prized for their glorious luster, iridescent orient, large size, and rainbow of natural colors. South Seas pearls grown in Australia are silvery white, rose white, and golden, depending on the species of oyster that produces the pearl.

Sometimes pearls are bleached, tinted, or washed with dye to enhance the color. This practice is very common with Japanese Akoya pearls, which are white, rose, and cream-colored. They are bleached even whiter and then washed with pink tint to give the desirable rose glow. Color alteration is standard practice for Japanese Akoya pearls, and it would be unusual to find a strand that has not been color-treated.

Types of Pearls

Natural

Since the invention a century ago of techniques for growing cultured pearls, few natural pearls have been found—perhaps one in tens of thousands. They are incredibly rare.

Akoya

Pristine, round, and pure, Japanese Akoyas are the pearl most recognized by consumers. The traditional white strand of four- to seven-millimeter Akoya pearls can be found in jewelry boxes around the world.

Chinese Freshwater

The freshwater pearls grown in the rivers and streams of China are the most abundant type of pearls in existence today. Grown in mussels, these pearls range in color from apricot to lavender, pink, cream, and white. It is possible to find a lovely freshwater pearl pendant or pair of earrings to fit any budget.

American Freshwater

Grown in rivers of the United States, mostly around the Mississippi River, these freshwater pearls are more rare than the Chinese version. From clear streams and rivers of the original Land of Pearls, as early explorers called it, these pearls are lustrous and beautiful as well as affordable.

Biwa

From Lake Biwa in Japan, the top of the line in freshwater pearls are Biwas. If you had the foresight to have purchased a Biwa pearl over the past fifty years, you have a treasure. There is now limited production of Biwa pearls due to the pollution of the lake.

South Seas

From Australia, these are the largest of all the types of pearls, ranging in size from twelve to sixteen millimeters. South Seas pearls are creamy white, lustrous, and expensive.

Tahitian

Exotic, iridescent, and rare, Tahitian pearls are created in a magical rainbow of colors. Often as large as their South Seas cousins, they are lustrous and in high demand.

Selecting Pearls

Most gem and jewelry lovers are far more educated about diamonds and other gems than they are about pearls, and often they lack confidence when making a purchase. Because this lack of understanding can be a detriment to the pearl producers, organizations such as World Pearl Organization, Cultured Pearl Association, Tahiti Pearl Association, Japan Pearl Promotion Society, and Australia's Licensed Pearl Producers are dedicated to informing consumers how to make an intelligent buying decision. They believe that the more the consumer learns about pearls, the more they will desire them.

When selecting pearls, always look first for luster. A high-luster pearl will show a sharp, bright reflection. Roll the pearl to see the luster on all sides. Or, if the pearl is set in a jewelry mounting, turn the piece in the light, looking at all sides of the pearl.

But consider all six of the criteria for evaluation and strike a balance between these factors. You may want the highest-quality luster and orient and be willing to settle for a smaller pearl. Or perhaps you will sacrifice some quality in luster or surface perfection to get a larger pearl.

Perfect pearls are rare. If the pearl is real, there will almost always be one or two beauty marks, either on the surface or within. Birthmarks and beauty marks that are not immediately visible to the naked eye are more acceptable than those that are. A pearl with chipped nacre, for example, would certainly be less acceptable.

If you have any doubt about the legitimacy of a pearl, try the tooth test by rubbing it gently along the top edge of your front bottom teeth. A genuine pearl will feel rough or sandpapery.

Educate yourself on the importance of each of the criteria, and then let your heart be your guide. Buying a pearl is ultimately a personal choice.

Pearl Strands

There are five well-known and accepted lengths for pearl necklaces. The following measurements are approximate.

The "choker" is usually 14 to 16 inches in length, lying just below the hollow of the neck; the "princess" is 16 to 20 inches in length; and the "matinée" is 20 to 26 inches long. "Opera" length is about 28 to 32 inches, and the "rope" is anything longer than opera length. Pearl strands can be either uniform in size or graduated. In uniform, the pearls are all the same size. In graduated, the pearls get increasingly large toward the center of the necklace. Graduated strands give the appearance of bigger pearls, because the largest are at the front of the necklace.

The pearls used in Akoya strands should match closely and blend together beautifully. When purchasing a pearl strand, it is a good idea to unclasp the ends, lay it straight on a white cloth, and roll the pearls back and forth. Rolling will reveal blemishes and inconsistencies in the pearls. Rolling will also allow you to check the pearls for luster, color, and match. It is normal for pearl strands to have some beauty marks. Remember, this is an organic gem of the sea, not a glass or plastic bead. Pearl strands should be restrung every one to two years, depending on how often they are worn. The pearls are strung on silk, with knots tied between each pearl, and these knots can stretch and fray.

Devin Macnow of the Cultured Pearl Information Center reports that for just one fine Akoya sixteen-inch necklace it takes over 640,000 painstaking man and oyster hours to grow enough pearls that are evenly matched in terms of luster, size, and color.

Caring for Pearls

Pearls are extremely durable when properly cared for, and their natural beauty is easy to maintain. They love the moisture and oil from the skin, so wearing your pearls also conditions them.

Pearls are precious gems and should be treated as such. Keep them in a satin, velvet, or chamois bag, separated from harder jewels that might scratch their surface.

Remember that pearls are produced by living organisms. Avoid contact with acidic substances, chlorine, and laundry or dishwashing detergents. Do not clean pearls with chemicals, abrasives, ammonia, or jewelry cleaners you would use for diamonds and harder gems; these substances are too abrasive. And be sure to put your pearls on *after* applying cosmetics, hair spray, or perfume.

The Gemological Institute of America recommends a gentle wash with warm fresh water to clean pearls effectively.

Occasionally give them a gentle wipe with a soft natural cloth such as a chamois. Wipe the pearl with a gentle downward motion, being careful not to twist it in its setting.

When well cared for, pearls can last many generations.

Suggested Reading

Pearls

Gems and Crystals. Anna S. Sofianides and George E. Harlow. New York: Simon & Schuster, 1990.

The Pearl Book: The Definitive Buying Guide. Antoinette L. Matlins. Woodstock, Vt.: GemStone Press, 2000.

Pearl Buying Guide. Renee Newman. Los Angeles: International Jewelry Publications, 1992.

Pearls. Shorei Shirai. Sault Sainte Marie, Mich.: Marine Publishing, 1981.

Pearls. Fred Ward. Bethesda, Md.: Gem Book Publications, 1995.

Pearls: A Natural History. Neil Landman, Paula Mikkelsen, Rudiger Bieler, and Bennet Bronson. New York: Harry N. Abrams, 2001.

Pearls: Ornament and Obsession. Kristin Joyce and Shellei Addison. New York: Simon & Schuster, 1993.

Pearls and Pearl Oysters. Shorei Shirai. Sault Sainte Marie, Mich.: Marine Publishing, 1994.

Perles de Tahiti. Jean Louis Saquet and Jean-François Dilhan. Papeete, Tahiti: Perles de Tahiti, 1997.

The Tahitian Pearl as Seen by Creative Jewelers. Didier Brodbeck. Papeete, Tahiti: G.I.E. (Groupement d'Interêt Economique) Perles de Tahiti, Dream Publications, 1997.

Personal Growth

The Artist's Way. Julia Cameron. New York: Jeremy P. Tarcher, 1992 (Audio edition: Putnam Publishing Group, 1997).

Chicken Soup for the Mother's Soul. Jack Canfield, Mark Victor Hansen, Jennifer Hawthorne, and Marci Shimoff. Deerfield Beach, Fla.: Health Communications, 1997 (Audio edition: Health Communications Audio, 1997).

Chicken Soup for the Surviving Soul. Jack Canfield, Bernie S. Siegel, and Patty Aubrey. Deerfield Beach, Fla.: Health Communications, 1996. (Audio edition: Health Communications Audio, 1998.)

Chicken Soup for the Woman's Soul. Jack Canfield and Mark Victor Hansen. Deerfield Beach, Fla.: Health Communications, 1996. (Audio edition: Health Communications Audio, 1996.)

End the Struggle and Dance with Life. Susan Jeffers. New York: St. Martin's Press, 1997. (Audio edition: Audio Renaissance, 1996.)

Feel the Fear and Do It Anyway. Susan Joffers. New York: Fawcett Books, 1992. (Audio edition: Simon & Schuster, 1994.)

Long Quiet Highway. Natalie Goldberg. New York: Bantam Doubleday Dell, 1994. (Audio edition: Sounds True, 1999.)

The Right to Write. Julia Cameron. New York: Jeremy P. Tarcher, 1999. (Audio edition: Audio Renaissance, 1999.)

Send Me Someone: A True Story of Love Here and Hereafter. Diana von Welanetz Wentworth. Los Angeles: Renaissance Books, 2001. (Audio edition: Audio Renaissance, 2001.)

Simple Abundance. Sarah Ban Breathnach. New York: Warner Books, 1995. (Audio edition: Time Warner AudioBooks, 1996.)

Simple Abundance Companion. Sarah Ban Breathnach. New York: Warner Books, 2000.

Succulent Wild Woman. Sark. New York: Fireside, 1997. (Audio edition: Audio Literature, 1997.)

The Vein of Gold. Julia Cameron. New York: Jeremy P. Tarcher, 1997.

Wild Mind. Natalie Goldberg. New York: Bantam Books, 1990. (Audio edition: Writer's AudioShop, 1996.)

Writing Down the Bones. Natalie Goldberg. Boston: Shambhala Publications, 1998. (Audio edition: Sounds True, 1999.)

Acknowledgments

 *T*housands of rainbow-colored pearls to my cherished husband, Don, who invited me to join him on his path of the pearl fourteen years ago. You are my inspiration and my muse, and your love heals me and fills me with joy.

The iridescent orient of love and spiritual blessings to my best friend and perfect partner, Diana von Welanetz Wentworth, for encouraging and supporting me along each step of this pearly path. You read the book countless times in all its many incarnations and always believed in me. And thanks to Ted Wentworth, for sharing Diana and trusting Don and me with your friendship and love.

Exotic rare pearls for Susan Crawford, my friend and literary agent, for standing by me during the more arduous segments of my path of the pearl. You are one in a million, the most rare and valuable.

Lustrous strands of gleaming pearls to Petra Halder-Nilsson, Pamela Schrack, Ron Imanaka, and the entire team at the Black Pearl Gallery Oahu and Maui stores as well as to Jan and Richard Amos and the BPG team Big Island and Lake Tahoe. Your spirit and commitment inspire me, your support gives me strength and energy, your love is the magic you give to everyone you meet as you share the pearls with the world.

Baroque pearls with fascinating shapes to freelance editors Ann Hartley and John Neindorff, who at different times in the book's evolution gave generously of their talent and time. Ann, you elegantly smoothed the edges and made them satiny. You gave this pearl its lustrous sheen and earned my undying respect and friendship. Your attention to detail is exquisite; and I loved the many months of late nights we spent together on the Internet.

Pearls of wisdom to all the talented people at Beyond Words Publishing who helped transform the writing into a gem of a book. Beyond Words pulses with nurturing energy; the creativity and skill contained in this one company is truly inspirational. Cynthia Black has lavished me with her creative genius, brainstorming the most inventive strategies for marketing my book. My delightful editor, Jenefer

Angell, gave her heart, exceptional skill, and strong sense of direction to the nurturing of this pearl. Jenefer, you were a joy to work with, and I deeply appreciate your talent and professionalism. Publisher Richard Cohn consistently thinks "outside the box" and is always inventing brilliant new ways to share books with the world.

Mahalo to John and Shannon Tullius, founders of the Maui Writers Conference, for creating the best writer's conference in the Universe, where I found my literary agent, Susan Crawford, and my publisher, Beyond Words.

Pearls of love to my family: Janet Whitehead, my infinitely loving and creative mother; Homer Olsen, my inspiring leader and mentor father; Barbara Curtis, my courageous and passionately supportive sister; Robert Olsen, my life-force-spark brother; and Donna, Kyle, Chuck, Joyce, Opal, Steve, Helen, Tom, Arne, Ann, Barbara, Anson, Ava, Ursula, and GW.

Pearls of gratitude to Don's family for loving and accepting me: Joan, Vicki, Steve, Sarah, Kris, Mike, Donna, Shane, Sharon, Luke, and John.

Pearls of mana to Serge Kahili King, Gloria King, and everyone at Aloha International for the wisdom, love, and support you share.

Pearls of healing to all the women at the Nu'uanu Reach for Recovery ACS support group for your love, courage, support, and beauty. Together we are all creating pearls from dire circumstances.

Pearls of unique shapes and sizes to all my dearest friends, from New York City, to Hollywood, to Hawaii, who have all contributed enormously to my life: Pam Arciero Lanza, Bobbie Probstein, Jody Mishan, Lolly Susi, Robert Stadd, Tim Piering, Heidi Lucas Page, Pauline Valha Miner, Sarah Hunter, Frank Clare, Tony and Chris Leone, and Pandora Kurth.

In the three years it has taken to create the pearl that is this book, I have been nurtured and assisted at every turn. My deepest gratitude to all who have been there for me. Our lives are shaped by the challenges we overcome—and the message of the pearl is this: "Whenever difficulties occur, it could be a pearl in the making."

Share Your Own "Pearl"!

Visit *www.pathofthepearl.com*

If you have an experience you would like to share with other women, send Mary Olsen Kelly your story, poem, or song about the ways you have taken the adversities of your life and created art and beauty.

Each month, one story will be selected to be featured on *www.pathofthepearl.com.*

Selections will be made on the fifteenth of each month and announced on the Web site the first day of the following month.

Visit our Web site to e-mail your story, or simply tear out or copy the form below and mail it in.

Name _____

Address _____

_____

Phone _____ Fax _____

E-mail address _____

Mail to
Path of the Pearl
Black Pearl Gallery
Ward Center
1200 Ala Moana Blvd.
Honolulu, Hawaii 96814

Our Turn, Our Time

Women Truly Coming of Age

Editor: Cynthia Black; Foreword: Christina Baldwin

$14.95, softcover

Our Turn, Our Time is an amazing collection of essays written by women who are committed to celebrating and valuing their passages into the second half of life. These women are redefining the role older women play in contemporary society by embracing creativity, spirituality, and sisterhood. These essays are filled with insight, humor, and compassion on a broad variety of topics: the richness of women's groups, the rewards of volunteering, the power of crone ceremonies, the fires of creative expression, the challenges of a changing body, and the confidence that comes from success in later life.

Rites of Passage

Celebrating Life's Changes

Authors: Kathleen Wall, Ph.D., and Gary Ferguson

$12.95, softcover

Every major transition in our lives—be it marriage, high-school graduation, the death of a parent or spouse, or the last child leaving home—brings with it opportunities for growth and self-actualization and for repositioning ourselves in the world. Personal ritual—the focus of *Rites of Passage*—allows us to use the energy held within the anxiety of change to nourish the new person that is forever struggling to be born. *Rites of Passage* begins by explaining to readers that human growth is not linear, as many of us assume, but rather occurs in a five-part cycle. After sharing the patterns of transition, the authors then show the reader how ritual can help him or her move through these specific life changes: work and career, intimate relationships, friends, divorce, changes within the family, adolescence, issues in the last half of life, and personal loss.

The Woman's Book of Dreams

Dreaming as a Spiritual Practice
Author: Connie Cockrell Kaplan; Foreword: Jamie Sams
$14.95, softcover

Dreams are the windows to your future and the catalysts to bringing the new and creative into your life. Everyone dreams. Understanding the power of dreaming helps you achieve your greatest potential with ease. *The Woman's Book of Dreams* emphasizes the uniqueness of women's dreaming and shows the reader how to dream with intention, clarity, and focus. In addition, this book will teach you how to recognize the thirteen types of dreams, how your monthly cycles affect your dreaming, how the moon's position in the sky and its relationship to your astrological chart determine your dreaming, and how to track your dreams and create a personal map of your dreaming patterns. Connie Kaplan guides you through an ancient woman's group form called dream circle—a sacred space in which to share dreams with others on a regular basis. Dream circle allows you to experience life's mystery by connecting with other dreamers. It shows you that through dreaming together with your circle, you create the reality in which you live. It is time for you to recognize the power of dreams and to put yours into action. This book will inspire you to do all that—and more.

Celebrating Time Alone

Stories of Splendid Solitude
Author: Lionel Fisher
$14.95, softcover

Celebrating Time Alone, with its profiles in solitude, shows us how to be magnificently alone through a celebration of our self: the self that can get buried under mountains of information, appointments, and activities. Lionel Fisher interviewed men and women across the country who have achieved great emotional clarity by savoring their individuality and solitude. In a writing style that is at once eloquent and down to earth, the author interweaves their real-life stories with his own insights and experiences to offer counsel, inspiration, and affirmation on living well alone.

The Infinite Thread

Healing Relationships beyond Loss
Author: Alexandra Kennedy
$14.95, softcover

The death of a loved one is often accompanied by regrets—for what we said or didn't say, what we did or didn't do. In our grief, our old resentments, regrets, and unexpressed love can hinder our emotional growth, creating wounds that affect all our other relationships. With exercises designed to re-create and heal past relationships, *The Infinite Thread* illustrates that keeping our loved one alive in our hearts—and in our minds—will enable us to make peace with the past and move freely into the future.

The Intuitive Way

A Guide to Living from Inner Wisdom

Author: Penney Peirce; Foreword: Carol Adrienne

$16.95, softcover

When intuition is in full bloom, life takes on a magical, effortless quality; your world is suddenly full of synchronicities, creative insights, and abundant knowledge just for the asking. *The Intuitive Way* shows you how to enter that state of perceptual aliveness and integrate it into daily life to achieve greater natural flow through an easy-to-understand, ten-step course. Author Penney Peirce synthesizes teachings from psychology, East-West philosophy, religion, metaphysics, and business. In simple and direct language, Peirce describes the intuitive process as a new way of life and demonstrates many practical applications from speeding decision-making to expanding personal growth. Whether you're just beginning to search for a richer, fuller life experience or are looking for more subtle, sophisticated insights about your spiritual path, *The Intuitive Way* will be your companion as you progress through the stages of intuition development.

The Art of Thank You

Crafting Notes of Gratitude

Author: Connie Leas

$14.96, hardcover

While reminding us that a little gratitude can go a long way, this book distills the how-tos of thank-yous. Part inspirational, part how-to, *The Art of Thank You* will rekindle the gratitude in all of us and inspire readers to pick up a pen and take the time to show thanks. It stresses the healing power that comes from both giving and receiving thanks and provides practical, concrete, and inspirational examples of when to write a thank-you note and what that note should include. With its appealing and approachable style, beautiful gift presentation, charming examples, and real-life anecdotes, *The Art of Thank You* has the power to galvanize readers' resolve to start writing their all-important thank-you notes.

Embracing the Goddess Within

A Creative Guide for Women

Author: Kris Waldherr

$17.95, hardcover

Embracing the Goddess Within continues the tradition of Kris Waldherr's best-selling *The Book of Goddesses*.

Exquisite, magical, and joyous, this glowing book resonates with the energy that for thousands of years has been summed up in the word *goddess*. *Embracing the Goddess Within* is divided into six sections that mirror the eternal feminine rites of passage: Beginnings, Love, Motherhood, Creativity, Strength, and Transformations. Each section contains a selection of goddesses for that particular stage or interest of a woman's life, giving her guidance for whatever challenge she faces. Each goddess is presented in a lyrical accounting of her myth accompanied by a beautiful illustration and simple ritual designed to invoke her spirit and power. Romantic, visually stunning, and as fun as it is practical, *Embracing the Goddess Within* is an essential addition to the personal library of all twenty-first-century goddesses.

Spiritual Writing
From Inspiration to Publication
Authors: Deborah Levine Herman with Cynthia Black
$16.95, softcover

Spiritual writers are drawn to the writing process by a powerful sense of mission. But that call to write is often at odds with the realities of publishing and the commercial needs of publishers. In *Spiritual Writing*, writer and literary agent Deborah Levine Herman and publisher Cynthia Black show writers how to create a book that both remains true to their vision and still conforms to the protocols of the publishing industry. Written with the intention of guiding and informing writers on their journey to publication, the book includes journaling exercises, tips on finding an agent and publisher, guidelines for writing query letters and proposals, a glossary of industry terms, and a comprehensive database that provides specifics on "spirit-friendly" publishers and agents.

The Widening Stream
The Seven Stages of Creativity
Author: David Ulrich
$16.95, softcover

Many people long for the fulfillment of their creative potential yet don't know how to attain it. Books on the subject are scientific and dense or idealistic and limited, often asserting that the creative impulse cannot be taught—that it is inherent in some people, like artists, writers, and scientists, and not in others. Using the stream as a metaphor, David Ulrich takes the reader through the seven steps of the creative process and shows that it's accessible to everyone.

Gracefully written and deeply resonant, *The Widening Stream* encourages readers to develop their innate artistic abilities, achieve their expressive aims, and find the courage and perseverance necessary to fulfill their deepest aspirations.

Your Authentic Self

Be Yourself at Work
Author: Ric Giardina
$14.95, softcover

Working people everywhere feel that they lead double lives: an "on the job" life and a personal life. Is it possible to live a life in which the separate parts of our personalities are united? In *Your Authentic Self*, author Ric Giardina explains that it is possible, and the key to achieving this integrated existence is authenticity. By honoring your authentic self at the workplace, you will not only be much happier, but you will also be rewarded with better on-the-job performance and more fulfilling work relationships. With straightforward techniques that produce instant results, this practical and easy-to-use guide will empower you to make the shift from seeing work as "off the path" of personal and spiritual growth to recognizing it as an integral part of your journey.

To order or to request a catalog, contact
Beyond Words Publishing, Inc.
20827 N.W. Cornell Road, Suite 500
Hillsboro, OR 97124-9808
503-531-8700

You can also visit our Web site at *www.beyondword.com*
or e-mail us at *info@beyondword.com*.

BEYOND WORDS PUBLISHING, INC.

OUR CORPORATE MISSION
Inspire to Integrity

OUR DECLARED VALUES
We give to all of life as life has given us.
We honor all relationships.
Trust and stewardship are integral to fulfilling dreams.
Collaboration is essential to create miracles.
Creativity and aesthetics nourish the soul.
Unlimited thinking is fundamental.
Living your passion is vital.
Joy and humor open our hearts to growth.
It is important to remind ourselves of love.